EVERY CHILD IS A GENIUS

Everybody is a Genius. But if you judge a fish by its ability to climb a tree, it will live its whole life believing that it is stupid.

—Albert Einstein

EVERY CHILD IS A GENIUS

Easy ways to awaken
child's potential

BRIG H R SHARMA

Published by:

PENTAGON PRESS

Marketed by:

MANJUL

Manjul Publishing House

First published in India by:

Pentagon Press,
206, Peacock Lane,
Shahpur Jat, New Delhi, INDIA - 110 049

Marketed by:
Manjul Publishing House Pvt. Ltd.
Corporate Office:
2nd Floor, Usha Preet Complex,
42 Malviya Nagar, Bhopal 462 003 - India
E-mail: manjul@manjulindia.com
Website: www.manjulindia.com
Marketing Office:
7/32, Ground floor, Ansari Road, Daryaganj, New Delhi - 110 002
Email: booksupplyco@manjulindia.com

Every Child is A Genius by ***Brigadier H R Sharma*** (Retd.)

This edition first published in 2013

ISBN 978-81-8274-686-2

Printed & bound in India by Thomson Press (India) Ltd.

Dedicated
to my
Mom and Dad

Preface

Every child is a genius. A world of potential resides within every child. If properly nurtured, this potential can blossom into something magnificent. In today's world, schools alone cannot give your child the tools necessary for success. To achieve excellence, your child needs your help. This book shows you how to do it.

'Every child is a genius' is a self help book which caters to the interest of both the parents and their child. They can guide their child and sow the seeds for his becoming a genius. Also, a child who wants to excel, can intelligently apply the suggested principles, techniques and tips. I assure you that you and your child will delight in the meaningful progress you will achieve together.

I will be delighted to answer your queries/ suggestions.

Happy reading.

Brigadier H R Sharma [Retd]
hakumat@hotmail.com

Contents

Acknowledgements

I would like to thank *Mr. Rajan Arya*, CEO, Pentagon Press and Colonel Harjeet Singh (Retd); who have inspired and guided me to write this book. I would also like to place on record my gratitude to my wife *Kusum,* my son *Dhruv,* and his wife Harpreet, and daughter *Sonali,* who not only encouraged me but also stood by me. This book would not have seen the light of the day without the assistance of my wonderful daughter, *Sonali.*

1

You Too, Can be a Genius, Just Know their Characteristics

"Genius is one per cent inspiration,
Ninety-nine per cent perspiration."

—Thomas A Edison

Genius means someone with exceptional talent and abilities, who has accomplished a few things more and have become famous. Albert Einstein qualifies for that, as does Edison.

This word is also used for someone who has a particular talent or skill. On this note we can say that Roger Federer is a genius with a tennis racquet and Lata Mangeshkar is a genius in the music field. It is also used to describe someone's skill. Sachin Tendulkar has cricketing genius in him.

I am sure you want to think and work like a genius. If

you look at the lives of the world's greatest geniuses like Edison, Socrates, Leonardo da Vinci, Shakespeare, Einstein, you will discover they all had many personality characteristics in common. Can the traits displayed by geniuses be developed? The answer is, YES. The traits can be developed by anyone. It makes no difference how old you are, how much education you have or what you have accomplished till date. Adopting personality characteristics mentioned below will enable you to operate on a genius level.

- Geniuses have the courage to do things that others consider impossible. They are willing to give all they have to a project. They know what they want and run after it and are sure of success. They continuously accumulate information and gain knowledge, understand the facts of a situation before concluding. They have an inquisitive and curious mind which helps them to seek new information. The more they learn to accomplish, the more confidence they develop. Further, they are optimistic, they overcome fear of failure and are not afraid to take chances. Geniuses are always excited about everything they do; it encourages others to co-operate with them.
- Geniuses are fully aware, that every problem can be solved in a surprising and creative way if they remain persistent enough over a consistent period of time. For this reason, they bring forth a resilient attitude towards every challenge confronting their reality.
- Geniuses are enterprising and great opportunity seekers. They are not afraid to try the unknown and can use their imagination. They know how to think in new combinations, and see things from a different

perspective. Geniuses are able to effectively get their ideas across to others. They are persuasive and know how to motivate people to help them get ahead.

- Geniuses believe in being perfect and cannot tolerate mediocrity. They always strive to do better, to achieve great things, not just for themselves, but for the betterment of mankind. Being flexible enables them to adapt to the changing circumstances readily and resist doing things in the same old way. They are always willing to consider new options.
- Geniuses approach every task or activity in the most curious manner. They fully believe that only curiosity and playfulness are able to relax their mind.

Living Geniuses of India

India is a land of talent and geniuses. There are a large number of people who make us feel proud. They are also role models to many. These people have excelled in their chosen fields, and truly measured up to the genius's class. Hard work, dedication, high level of motivation, coupled with the ability to face set backs or failures, are their forte. They have abundance of positive qualities of head and heart, and are revered by millions.

Who is your favourite sports person? Sachin Tendulkar is known as the "Master Blaster," and is an international cricket player. Saina Nehwal is number two in world ranking in badminton, and is likely to be come number one soon. Our brainy boy, Vishawanathan Anand, is a world champion in chess and is one of the most famous sports personality of India. The list is long; you may like to add names of your favourites.

In the field of music and singing, who has not heard the melodious songs of Lata Mangeshkar? Recently, A R Rehman won an Oscar award for music. In the classical field, Pandit Ravi Shankar and many other artists have mesmerized millions of people throughout the world.

Who does not know Amartya Sen? He is a world famous economist and has been awarded the Nobel Prize.

There are many geniuses in field of politics and religion. Not only this, there are so many intellectuals and scientists living in India who have not been mentioned here, primarily due to lack of space.

Why We Live as Long as We Do?

One day God created a cow. God said, "You must go to the fields with the farmer for the whole day and suffer under the sun, have calves and give milk to support the farmer. I will give you a life span of sixty years."

The cow said, "That's a tough life you want me to live, for sixty years. Let me have twenty; and I'll give back the other forty." And God agreed.

On the second day, God created a dog. God said, "Sit all day by the door of your house and bark at anyone who comes in or walks past. I will give you a lifespan of twenty years."

The dog said, "That's too long for barking. Give me ten years; I'll give back the other ten." So God agreed. On the third day, God created a monkey. God said, "Entertain people, do monkey tricks, make them laugh. I'll give you a twenty year lifespan."

The monkey said, "How boring! Monkey tricks for twenty years? I don't think so. Dog gave you back ten, so that's what I'll do too, okay?" And God agreed again.

On the fourth day, God created man. God said, "Eat, sleep, play. Do nothing, just enjoy, enjoy. I'll give you twenty years."

Man said, "What? Only twenty years? No way! Tell you what, I'll take my twenty and the sixty given back by the cow, dog and monkey. That makes a total of eighty years, okay?"

"Okay," said God, "You have got a deal."

So that is why for the first twenty years we eat, sleep, play, enjoy, and do nothing.

For the next forty years we slave in the sun to support our family.

For the next ten years we do monkey tricks to entertain our grandchildren.

In the last ten years, we sit and make ourselves miserable by thinking about the time we lost in doing insignificant things, and carry a heavy baggage full of grudges and missed opportunities.

We are born genius with a brilliant brain which is capable of empowering us with super potential. Think, what we do during the years gifted to us by the God!

2

Do Personal Analysis to Know Yourself

"Knowing yourself is the beginning of all wisdom."

—Aristotle

Knowing yourself, is the key ingredient for becoming a genius. Do you know what are you good at? What you love doing and what energizes you? What things upsets you and makes you feel in a soup? If the answer to these questions is yes, Congratulations, you are on the right track.

Knowing yourself will enable you to develop your full potential and feel happy, contented and fulfilled. Knowing yourself and working on changing for the better will enable you to achieve your goals. You will turn out to be much happier and that would be a success in a true sense.

Genius people know that the responsibility for making their lives work, lies within them. They trust themselves and rely on their own judgment. While working on knowing yourself, here are few techniques to help you.

- Take out a moment to write down things that you know "very nicely", and "not so nicely" about yourself—your interests, likes, dislikes, preferences, hobbies, strengths, weaknesses, hopes, fears, dreams, etc. Reflect on these qualities and find out how they impact your overall life.

- You could also know yourself better by understanding people's perceptions about you. Pay attention to what your family, friends, class mates, observe and say about you.
- Another way to know yourself is to take personality and psychological tests. By answering them, you will understand more how you think, take decisions, interact with people, do things, choose friends, live your life, etc.
- Carry out **SWOT analysis**, which means **Strengths, Weaknesses, Opportunities, and Threats.** These identifications will help you to know yourself. Thereafter, take actions to achieve your desired goals.

SWOT Analysis

Identify your Strengths

You need to be aware of your personal strengths. The answers to the following questions will help you to identify your strengths:

- What are you good at?
- Where lies your greatest area of knowledge?
- What personal qualities do you have?
- What makes you unique?
- What is there in you that you don't want to change?

List Your Weaknesses

You need to be aware of your weaknesses so that you can

improve them. Beware of comparisons; the quickest way to deflate your spirits is to compare yourself with other people, especially the wrong ones. To know your weaknesses, write down answers to the following:

- What do you consider to be your weaknesses?
- Where does your knowledge lack?
- What qualities do you miss?
- Which aspects of yourself, you find hard to accept?
- What do you want to change?

Identify the Opportunities

Your aim in identifying opportunities is to recognize areas which needs further development. These could include personal attributes, qualifications, experiences, health and fitness, communication skills, etc. Start thinking about your strengths. For each strength jot down points how you could make better use of it in the future. Then consider:

- What opportunities do you have right now?
- What other opportunities can you create, if you develop a particular strength or work on a weakness?
- What have you overlooked?

Threats

What will be the consequences of remaining as you are? Which of your goals will be most at risk? From where, what or from whom do the threats come? If you're still not sure about your strengths and weaknesses, get some feedback from others. Ask them, what in their opinion, you need to develop and what you can do to improve. If they say something you disagree with, find out more about this view. When they have finished, thank them. In your Self-Coaching

Journal write down.

- What did you learn about yourself from this exercise?
- What will you do differently as a result of this exercise?
- What was good about their feedback?

Quiz: Know Yourself

Look at each of the following statements and encircle what closely relates to your answer.

Can you tell when your mood is changing?

A. Always
B. Sometimes
C. Rarely
D. Never

Do you know when you are becoming defensive?

A. Always
B. Sometimes
C. Rarely
D. Never

Can you tell when your emotions are affecting your performance?

A. Always
B. Sometimes
C. Rarely
D. Never

How quickly do you realize that your thoughts are turning negative?

A. Immediately
B. Quiet soon
C. After a while
D. Usually too late

How quickly do you realize that you are going to lose your temper?

A. Very Quickly
B. Not very quickly
C. Slowly
D. Very slowly

Scoring: Give yourself 4 points if you have encircled A; 3 points for B; 2 points for C and 1 point for D. Add up to get your total score for knowing your level of self-awareness.

17 or above – well done

13 to 16 – you need to do some work

12 to 9 – you need to do a lot of work

8 or below – you need to work hard to 'know yourself'.

Are You a Winner or a Loser?

Winner explains and a loser explains anyway. A winner says, "Let's find a way", a loser says, "There is no way."

A winner goes through a problem; a loser tries to go around it. A winner says, "There should be a better way to do it"; a loser says, "That's the way it's always been done here."

A winner knows what to fight for and where to compromise; a loser compromises on what he or she should not, and fights for what is not worth fighting for.

A winner works harder than anyone else, and has more time; a loser is always "too busy" to do what is necessary. A winner is never afraid of losing; a loser is secretly afraid of winning. A winner makes commitments; a loser makes promises.

3

Aim for Core Desires which Inspire You

"Arise, awake and stop not till the goal is reached."

—***Swami Vivekananda***

Here is a fascinating story of grit, determination and will power to excel in spite of having major physical disabilities.

Wilma Rudolph's mother was told by the doctors that her daughter would never be able to walk again. Refusing to believe that her child could never walk again, her mother took her to the hospital for the bi-weekly physiotherapy sessions religiously. Every session was a painful experience but Wilma persisted on, believing in her mother when she said she could walk again. It was her belief that enabled her to start walking a few years later. She went on to become the first American woman in history to win three Olympic gold medals in a row.

When she was six, Wilma Rudolph was given metal braces to aid her in walking. Though the braces were supposed to help her, she hated them. To her, those were chains that imprisoned her at home and kept her away from school. It was during this time that she became literally frustrated with life's adversity and swore to herself that she would fight the disease no matter what it might take.

When she was in primary school, she joined the basketball team. Despite her pleas to play, Wilma remained a reserve for three full years and watched, observed and analyzed the game. Until she became probably as good as her coach! In her fourth year with the team, she made an appeal to be in the starting lineup and when her wish was finally granted, she dazzled everyone by leading the team to an undefeated season of the state championships. Though they lost the championship title, Wilma Rudolph earned the attention of the women's track coach and was invited to join the "Tiger belles", a premier women's track & field's team in the region. At that time, she was only a high school student. Joining "Tiger belles" gave her a different perspective.

It stimulated her competitive nature and sprung her into action, making her work with her coach closely and picking up the breathing techniques and racing strategy. She built up her stamina and physical strength. At the same time, her mindset also changed. No longer idolizing her track seniors as heroes, she allowed herself to beat their timings. She made it to the Rome Olympics to compete in three separate events. Although she suffered from a sprained ankle but she did not let it affect her performance. She shocked the world by winning and breaking the world record. Wilma Rudolph's extraordinary achievements in Rome, made her a darling of the European press who gave her the nicknames "The Black Gazelle" and "The Black Pearl". Indisputably, she became the first woman in American history to win three gold medals in the Olympics and was crowned "The Fastest Woman in the World".

What can you learn from Wilma Rudolph? It is a great reminder to us that we can overcome life's adversity with determination and sheer will power. To succeed in life, believe in yourself and learn from your failures. Wilma had set goals for herself at each stage of her life and took action to achieve them. She was persistent in her efforts. She wanted to walk like every kid on the block, so she worked on her therapy exercises and practised walking without the braces. She wanted to be in the starting lineup for the basketball team, and so she honed her techniques and acquired her coach's analytical skills and fought for an opportunity to perform. She wanted to win a gold medal for her races in the 1960 Olympics and hence, she followed a four year intensive training schedule. Four years! How many of us give up at facing failures after a few months of our working on something we want to achieve?

Why do we need to set goals like Wilma had done for herself? If we desire success in life, we need to set goals like Wilma did. There is a direct link between goals and enhanced performance. What is a goal? A goal is an objective and a purpose of life. It is more than a dream and can be stated as a dream acted upon. Achievements in sports events, computer technology, warfare, etc. are goals inspired. If somebody asks you, "what is so great about setting a goal?" What will be your response? You could respond by stating that when we set a goal, it gives us a target to aim at and automatically our effort gets directed towards attainment of our core desire.

How to Set Goals?

Those who have the courage to dream big and conviction to turn them into reality comes out successful. For instance, Mr. Dhirubhai Ambani started off with meagre resources but through sheer grit and hard work, he established a huge industrial empire. Similarly, Henry Ford who founded Ford Motor Company began his life as a poor boy, but with sheer hard work, became the richest American of his days. At the age of 16, Henry Ford worked for 14 hours a day to earn about 5 dollars. But he did not give up and strived hard to achieve his goal in life. These two success stories amply clearifies that hard work plays an important role in achievement of goals. If you want to succeed, set goals that command your thoughts, liberates your energy and inspires your hopes. To set goals remember an acronym, "SMART", which stands for the following:—

Specific

The goal must be action oriented and specific. Example: I want to be a mechanical engineer. Goal must be well defined, clear and unambiguous.

Measurable

The goal should be easily measurable. Instead, of saying I want to be rich, you should define how much wealth will make you rich. Example: I want to be rich and earn one hundred billion. It means that the goal should be such that your progress towards achieving it can be measured.

Achievable

It should be within your reach, though you may have to stretch a bit. We can say that goal must be ambitious but achievable. Example: one should not aim to buy a property on the moon.

Relevance

It should be relevant to self and to the society. It should also be in line with your beliefs and values. Example: I want to become a doctor and help the poor sick people.

Time Limit

Decide a deadline by which the goal is to be accomplished.

Clearly defined time frame includes the starting date and a target date. Napoleon Hill says, *"A goal is a dream with a deadline"*. Example: I will own my own company by 35 years of age.

Rahul Gandhi is a young man with great charismatic aura and vision. He is one of the new rays of hope in the world of Indian politics. Like any other young man, he loves speed. His choice of machines ranges from Kawasaki Ninjas and Yamaha R1s to dirt bikes and even karts. He says, "My heart beats for India..." His view on the need to focus on goals is, "We believe that we should remain focused on our target and strive towards achieving it."

Remember, if you desire success and happiness in life, set goals. They give a target to aim at and direction to head towards. Once you are clear about your goals in life, you should make plans to achieve them.

A bit of humour at this stage will surely brighten up things

A man, who had just died, arrived at heaven's gate. Before allowing him to enter, St. Peter asked him if he'd ever loved a woman.

"No", the man replied, "Not a single one..."

"Did you have a friend you cared for?"

"No".

"Perhaps you loved a pet? Did you feel a love for nature?"

"No".

"What took you so long to get here?" asked St. Peter. "You have been dead for ages..."

Did the above mentioned person have a goal in life? Would he have lived a full life even if he was the President of a country?

4

Wake Up to Realize Your Goals

"Setting goals is the first step
In turning the invisible into the visible."

—Anthony Robbins

Have you seen the movie, "Rocket Singh?" It's about a young man, a modern day dreamer who wants to realize his goal in the shortest time. There is nothing wrong in thinking big, but the methods used must be fair and ethical. To exemplify what I have just stated, here is a beautiful story, title as, "Think, Believe, Dream and Dare."

A young boy approached an old man in front of a wishing well, looking up into his eyes, said, "I understand you are a very wise man. I would like to know the secret of life." The old man looked down at the youngster and replied, "I have thought a lot in my lifetime, and the secret can be summed up in four words, **"Think, Believe, Dream and Dare."**

- Think about the values as per which you wish to live your life.
- Believe in yourself and base it on the values you have chosen for yourself to lead your life.
- Dream about the things that are based on your beliefs and the values.

- Dare to make your dreams a reality, based on your self-belief and values."

Why do we set goals?

The basic reason for setting a goal is to achieve a desired outcome. Capt. Gopinath, Chairman, Deccan Airlines, says, "To seek opportunities where others can't and then risking everything, is what it calls for to make my dream a reality. When I decided to launch Air Deccan, every analyst and market experts told me that the idea would not work in India. However, I proved them wrong". This is an excellent example of setting goals and working towards their achievement. Thomas Jefferson's views on achievement of goals are, "Nothing can stop a man with the right attitude from achieving his goal; nothing on earth can help a man with the wrong attitude". Pursuit of goals will become easier, if you follow the under mentioned rules.

- **Confidence in Ability to Achieve Goal.** Learn new skills and work on your abilities wholeheartedly. Psychologists are of the opinion that if you constantly think of success, it gets implanted in the subconscious mind which arouses you from slumber. Roger Barrister who first broke the four minute barrier in 1954 said that he constantly imagined breaking the record over and over in his mind. He visualized himself crossing the barrier with so much of emotional intensity that his body, mind and soul were programmed to carry it out. Remember, a major factor to achieve success in any endeavour is the ability to be completely free from anxiety, apprehension and doubt.

- Hard work and focus are the keys to the achievement of a goal. There is no substitute for hard work. Margaret Thatcher, former PM of England, once said "I do not know anyone who has got to the top without hard work. You must focus on the goal to be achieved". In Mahabharata, contestants were required to shoot an arrow in the eye of a bird. When asked what they were seeing, all of them started giving long explanations. But Arjun, who was totally focused, replied, "I see the eye of the bird and nothing else". This should be your level of focus in whatever you do. Napoleon, when he was a lieutenant, used to spend his spare time in studying artillery, how to lay siege and other related subjects.

Napoleon described how he worked in the following words, "I am always at work, I think a great deal. If I appear equal to any occasion, it is because I have thought over matters long before I undertake to do the slightest thing, I have foreseen all eventualities. There exists no guardian angel who suddenly and mysteriously whispers in my ears what I have to do. Everything is turned over in mind, again and again. At night I wake up to work."

- Progress towards the goal is hampered mainly by two factors, failures and problems on the path. Thomas Alva Edison went broke before finding the filament for the incandescent lamp as he had many failures in his experiments. When he was interviewed by a young reporter who asked him how he felt about thousands of failed experiments the scientist is reported to have replied, *"You are too young to understand that I have not had 9999 failures, I may have had that many experiments, but it simply means that I'm getting closer to finding the right solution, by ruling out 9999 that won't work."* It is generally seen that people give up when they are on the verge of success. Failures need to be taken as stepping-stones for success.

Everybody loves success. Here are true success stories of two very ordinary human beings, which inspire us to believe that we can achieve anything once we decide what we want and thereafter, pursue it vigorously with total focus and dedication.

Sunder Lal, a poor man, qualifies for IAS on his own merit. Sunder Lal, who resides in Panchkula Haryana, has scripted a big success story. A teacher in a Government High School, he ranked 731 in the elite IAS examination, held in 2008. He worked hard and did not waiver from his determination to clear the IAS exam. Sunder Lal was so poor, that he could not even afford to buy books. He used to borrow books and sometimes, his brother used to buy them for him. It's a great achievement as he did not take any formal coaching. Sunder Lal, when he was just 12 years old, lost his hearing power due to an alleged negligence of a doctor. He is still under treatment and has lost 60 per cent of his hearing power. He says, "I had problems initially, but I never lost heart. I wanted to excel. Now I want to serve the society." This is a true success story of someone who did not give up in spite of so many constraints and was stead fast in his pursuit of his goal. Just like him, "you too can". John Milton, Helen Killer and so many other people you may have heard of, have achieved great heights, in spite of having major disabilities as they were determined to succeed.

Rash Pal Kaur, a blind person, wants to achieve her goal. The other day I heard from one of my friends that Rash Pal

Kaur lost her eyesight in 2007 but has not given up dancing. She says, "Since childhood dance is a singular source of joy for me. It is the belief in me, which keeps me going". Counting her steps, keeping in mind the dimension of the stage and paying extra attention to the musical beats is how she performs. Her zeal and enthusiasm towards life is really an example of solid resolve to achieve the goal she has set for herself. We should be proud of such gifted people and wish them great success and happiness ahead.

Remember, goals have to be pursued with vigour and total dedication. Have confidence in your ability to achieve the desired goals. Hard work is the key to success. Be ready to face failures. Read success stories of people who, in spite of facing various challenges and failures, have been able to achieve their goals.

Here is a conversation between a doctor and a person whose aim is to live a hundred years.

Patient: Doctor, do you think that I will live until I am hundred?

Doctor: Do you smoke or drink?

Patient: No.

Doctor: Do you drive fast cars, gamble, or support a family?

Patient: Certainly not!

Doctor: Then what for do you want to live a hundred?

The best way to make your dream come true is to wake up.

—Paul Valery

5

Time is Your Precious Resource

"Take care of the minutes and the hours will take care of themselves."

—Lord Chesterfield

The concept of time management is much more important today than it was in the past. We live in a fast paced world where information moves at the speed of light, and people are working harder and longer. Time is one of the most valuable resources for achieving success. Many people take time for granted and undervalue it. Everyone, no matter how rich or poor, intelligent or ignorant, has the same 24 hours a day. Both, the CEO and a peon in an office, have an equal amount of time at their disposal. What matters is how it is managed to produce quality results. *"Time and Tide Wait for None"*, time is a paradox. We never seem to have enough time, yet we have all the time. You may have heard many people cribbing about the shortage of time. The real problem is that they do not examine their behaviour and habits, which are responsible for consuming most of their time. Remember, you can't control time, but you can always manage it. The key to manage time is to look at your involvement in various activities and thereafter, allot adequate time to each one of them depending upon their importance and urgency.

Assess Your Time Management Ability

Against the statements given below, please mark Never, Occasionally or Always.

- I arrive on time and come well prepared.
- I prepare "Daily to-do list".
- I reserve some time for my personal development.
- I am well organized and believe in delegation.
- I set for myself long and short-term goals.
- I make deliberate decisions.
- I care for my friends.
- I easily forgive.
- I understand the problem before taking decisions.
- I help the needy people.

Scoring: Give 3 marks for Always, 2 marks for Occasionally and 1 mark for Never. Add your total.

25 or above marks:	Your time management ability is above average
20 to 24 marks:	It is average.
Less than 20 marks:	Greater effort is required on your part to manage time.

Here is an interesting illustration on time management. One day, an expert in time management was speaking to a group of business students about the importance of time management. As he stood in front of the group of powerful and overachievers he said, "Okay, time for a quiz", and he pulled out a big jar and placed it on the table in front of him. He also produced about a dozen fist-sized rocks and carefully placed them, one at a time, into the jar. When the jar was filled to the top and no more rocks would fit inside, he asked the students, whether the jar was full. Everyone in the class replied, "Yes." The time management expert asked, "Really?" He reached under the table and pulled out a bucket of gravel. He dumped some gravel in and shook the jar causing the pieces of gravel to work for themselves down into the spaces between the big rocks. The expert then asked the group once more, "Is the jar full?" "Probably not," one of them answered. He reached under the table and brought out a bucket of sand. He started dumping the sand in the jar, and it went into all the spaces left between the rocks and the gravel. Once more, he asked the question, "Is this jar full?" "No!" the class shouted. Then he grabbed a pitcher of water and began to pour it in until the jar was filled to the brim.

Then he looked at the class and asked, "What is the point of this illustration?" One eager student raised his hand and said, "The point is, no matter how full your schedule is, if you try really hard you can always fit some more things in it!" "No," the speaker replied, "that's not the point. The truth this illustration teaches us is, if you do not put the big rocks first, you'll never get them in at all." What are the 'big rocks' in your life; time with your loved ones, your faith, your education, your dreams, teaching or mentoring others? Remember to put these big rocks in first or you'll never get them in at all. So, when you are reflecting on this short story, ask yourself this question: What are the big rocks in my life? Then put those in the jar first.

Pay-Offs for Being Time Effective

Managing time well has a number of pay-offs. Important tasks can be completed well in time with a lot of energy. It increases your ability to achieve more during the available time and people start respecting you. In addition, there is enough time to develop your personality and lead a stress free life.

Time is one of the most valuable resources for achieving success. Remember, managing time well has a number of pay-offs. You will get respect from people, have enough time to relax and take up activities you like.

This is what happens, when you don't manage time.

6

How to Manage Time Effectively?

"If you want to make good use of time, you have got to know what's most important and then give it all you have got."

—Lee Iaccoca

We are aware that time is a precious resource and it has to be managed. Good time management is not required just for work; it's required throughout your life. Manage your time well, and you will well manage your life too. The secret lies in managing time in an effective manner. Some ways of effective time management are:—

Read or Rewrite Goals

To achieve goals you must read or rewrite goals after every few months and make a progress report. Ensure that you do activities related to your chosen goals. Continually, try to eliminate unnecessary tasks which are not related to your goals or do not help in maintaining a balanced life-style. You should set deadlines to what you want to achieve. Once you set the deadline, you will start your project on time and there will be no panic at the last moment. You will soon find that you have mastered an important secret to increase productivity.

Avoid Time Wasters

You should identify time wasters. Thereafter, you must take action, manage and avoid them. Towards this direction, you could shorten your television watching period, stop procrastinating, organize your life, start tackling/doing important tasks and so on.

Learn to Say 'NO'

One of the primary causes of time pressure is our inability to say 'NO'. We feel that if we say 'NO' it may hurt the other person or it may lead to loss of friendship. Learn to say 'NO'; however, you need to soften the effect of 'NO' tactfully.

Remember the 80:20 Rule

The Pareto principle (also known as the 80:20 rule) states that, for many events, roughly 80% of the effects comes from 20% of the causes. It is named after Italian economist Wilfred Pareto, who observed that 80% of income in Italy went to 20% of the population. It is a common rule of thumb in business; i.e., 80% of your sales come from 20% of your clients." Even if the 80:20 rule is partially true, imagine what would happen if you start spending time and effort for the less effective 20%. Simply stated, it means 1% more effective action can produce 5% more results. Students can apply this principle, when they do revision before the examinations.

Delegate

Learn to delegate less important work to others and personally handle important issues. Effective delegation is the key to self management. When delegating, ensure that you delegate to the right person. Place resources and give out clear guidelines to ensure successful outcome. Have you noticed how she delegates.

Priorities

Some tasks don't require your best effort. For example, sending a short email to a friends, should not take more than a few minutes. Learn to distinguish between tasks that deserve to be done excellently and tasks that just need to be done. When you have so many tasks to do, there is a need to lay down priorities based on urgency and importance of the task. Look at the table below. You can see that you need to spend maximum time on priority 1 tasks and least on priority 4 tasks.

PRIORITY 1 Urgent and Important	**PRIORITY 2** Important but Not Urgent
PRIORITY 3 Urgent but Not Important	**PRIORITY 4** Not Important Nor Urgent

Develop Time Management Habit

Estimate the time needed for things you have to do. Do keep some cushion. Focus on leaving time and not arrival time. Suppose you have to attend a meeting at 3 p.m., in that case you must leave by 2:30 p.m. to get to a 3:00 p.m. meeting. Focus all your efforts to leave by 2:30 p.m. Avoid 'one last thing' tendency. When it is time to leave, don't try to make one more call, handle one more question or write one more memo. Trying to squeeze one more task will often make you late.

Spend Quality Time with Your Family

Decide an activity, based on these three questions: Does it involve active participation of the family? Does it draw family together? Does it produce a feeling of happiness and satisfaction for all? When you watch TV with your family, do you consider it spending quality time with them? Think about it.

Combine Certain Tasks

Certain tasks can be combined and done simultaneously. However, keep in mind the safety aspects. Some of the tasks which can be combined are like listening to music or motivational tapes while driving or reading a newspaper while travelling in a bus.

Make a List of Bad Habits

Identify habits that are stealing your time, sabotaging your goals, and blocking your success. After having done so, work on them, one at a time, and systematically eliminate them from your life. Remember that the easiest way to eliminate a bad habit is to replace it with a good habit.

Preparation of a 'To-do list'

Identify what is required to be done for the day, allot priorities and time required for completion. Focus on important tasks and don't waste time on trivial matters. When you have a 'to-do list' filled with important tasks, be careful about not getting distracted by "filler" tasks. Things such as organizing your bookcase or filing papers can wait until you complete the items that have the highest priority.

The importance of 'to-do list' is aptly demonstrated by the advice given to a steel magnate. Charles Schwab, when he was alive, was the richest man on the planet. He was most successful in running a steel empire. One day, somebody came up to him and said, "Mr. Schwab, I will give an idea and I would like you to use it for one month. At the end of the month you pay me whatever you think it was worth for". In the eyes of Schwab it looked as fair deal. Can you guess what was that idea?

Simple: At the end of each day write down the five most important things you should do tomorrow. What's the real secret? When you get up that day, you make sure those five things are done. If you only get through four, don't sweat. Number one on the list for the next day is already taken. Actions get things done and that makes the difference.

How much money did Mr. Schwab pay to the person who gave the idea? What's your guess? Well, Mr. Schwab paid one million dollars as he thought that the idea was well worth what he was paying.

Time Management Plan

To achieve success, there is need to make a time management plan. The plan is prepared keeping in mind various activities required to achieve short and long term goals. The plan could be prepared on a yearly or half yearly basis for larger organisations. It could be prepared on a quarterly or monthly basis for smaller organisations. It could include major tasks to be achieved along with deadlines. The plan must be simple and implementable. You must lay emphasis on those tasks which lead to maximum output.

In a nutshell, time is a precious resource and it must be managed effectively. Time can not be borrowed, begged, stolen, nor can it be deposited in a bank. Lost time never comes back. Time favours none and every one has the same number of hours in a day. I would like to say that ***Time is life***.

7

Think and Believe That You are a *Great* Person

"If you don't run your own life, somebody else will."
—*John Atkinson*

You don't have to guess, genius people ***Think and Believe*** that they are great. They value and respect themselves. ***Do You?*** If the answer is "no", please read carefully, and if it is 'yes', read more carefully.

People, who think and believe that they are great, work hard and live a better life. You can say they have a high level of self-esteem. Building high level of self-esteem is the first step towards happiness and greatness. Great people are confident and have a positive attitude towards life. You have a choice to be great or just an ordinary person. ***I Know, Your Choice is__________.***

A strong, positive self-esteem in young people is associated with being more assertive, with better physical health, with more satisfying relationships, and with an increasing ability to tolerate and accept differences in others.

Great people have a high sense of self-esteem. What makes self-esteem such an elusive idea is that it is so central to our feelings. It provides the medium through which everything else is experienced, like seeing the world through a coloured or self-doubting filter. It is perhaps not surprising. Therefore, the origin of our self-esteem goes back to our childhood. Warm, intimate and continuous attachments during childhood provide the kind of "emotional baggage" that helps to build self-esteem. This is provided by parents as well as others. But it is not only our childhood which is important but our experiences in adult life, especially those involving warm relationships with others, are also important sources of self-esteem. However, those who reach adulthood with low self-esteem can not remain stuck in a deadend. They can take many steps towards feeling better.

Quiz: Assess Your Level of Self-esteem

Here is a quiz to assess your level of self-esteem. Mark True or False against each of the statements given below.

- I accept myself as I am.
- I enjoy socializing.
- I feel valued and needed.
- I make friends easily.
- I can accept criticism without feeling low.
- I admit my mistakes openly.
- I'm a happy and carefree person.
- I don't need approval of others to feel good.

Assessment: For each 'True' answer give one point and none for 'False'. What is your total score?

7–8 points:	You have a high level of self-esteem.
5–6 points:	Your self-esteem is not bad but requires improvement.
5 or less points:	Your self-esteem is low; you need to work hard on it.

How we feel and value ourselves should not depend on others.

Let me tell you an interesting story. A young lady named Suman, had been divorced for about five years. She believed that she was ready for a new dating relationship in her life but nothing had worked for her. Something was holding her back. One of her friends suggested to her that may be her exhusband was still holding too much power over her emotions to allow her to engage in a relationship with someone else. She thought about that and realized that what really had happened was that when her husband had an affair with a much younger woman, her self-esteem was shaken totally. What advice will you give to Suman?

Well, you could tell her, "When our trust is shattered, we tend to look at ourselves. What's wrong with me? Why did someone I love betray me? Why didn't I see it? Instead, we need to look at the character flaw in the other person. When someone makes a promise to you and breaks it, then that is a flaw in him, not in you. The most important thing is not to lose respect for yourself. You are a worthy person. Spend some time engaging in some self-nurturing behaviour. Learn to love yourself again."

If you want to think great and believe in it too, ponder and write your views to the following questions:

- How well you do your studies? What is the importance of this job and what status it gives to you?
- Your achievements.
- How do you think others see you? How do you see yourself?
- Your strengths and weaknesses.
- Your social status and how you relate to others.
- Your independence or ability to stand on your feet.
- Can you make your own decisions? How do you live your life?
- How do you feel? Have you answered the questions? Are you feeling good? Is your level of self-esteem on top?

How do you rate Albert 's level of Self-esteem?

"Get up," shouted Albert's mother." You will be late for school..."

"But I don't want to go," protested Albert.

"All the kids are horrible, the teachers are terrible, and it is all extremely boring. I want to stay at home."

"But," replied Albert's mother, "you're fortythree and the headmaster of the school."

"Self-esteem is the evaluation which
An individual makes and customarily
Maintains with regard to him or herself,
It expresses an attitude of approval or
Disapproval towards oneself."

—Morris Rosenberg

Teacher: "Rocky, put your hand in one pocket and pull out a Rs. 500 note, then you put your hand in the other pocket and pull out another Rs. 500 note. What will you say?"

Rocky promptly replies, "Well Madam, I must be wearing somebody else's pants."

How do you rate Rocky's self-esteem?

8

How to Build Greatness in Your Life?

"Genius is a long impatience."

—Paul Clandel

There was a young boy who had lived with his grandmother, since he was just a few years old. He had no self-confidence; and his self-image was destroying him. Other people sensed that he had little self-confidence, particular his school bully who thrashed him severly very often. One day the young boy turned on the bully and knocked him on the ground. That year was 1670. This story is not to illustrate why or how he turned, it is more to show what happened after he turned. Within minutes the boy had a new 'self-image'. Within a few weeks, he was ahead of the class and in the next term, he was selected as the head boy of his school. Years later, he was knighted and became Sir Isaac Newton, discoverer of one of the most important universal laws. From the above incident, we learn that at times an incident can transform a person, especially when it has a positive effect, resulting in high self-esteem. It is important for you to always think that

you are a wonderful, worthwhile, capable and lovable person. Never take things too seriously or personally. Regularly take up challenges and act in accordance with your values.

Here are few techniques given by which you can build greatness in your life.

Stop Comparing Yourself with Others

Do you compare yourself with others and try to find out your shortcomings? STOP. There are always some people better than you. Accept this fact. It is much better to accept yourself as who you are and what you look like and don't waste energy and happiness in trying to be like someone else. Think of the child who rushes proudly home from school saying: "I came second in class." "Who came first?", asks the parents and the child retires crushed. Avoid negative phrases about yourself and your abilities. Instead, make a positive formation about yourself, such as.

- I'm the best.
- I feel great.
- I can do it.
- I can solve it.
- Today is going to be a great day.
- I'm successful.
- I'll pass.
- It is possible.
- I look great.

Bury the Prejudice

Low self-esteem is like a prejudice about oneself as being

unworthy, or unacceptable. The self perception is biased or flawed, but the person with the prejudice has a hard time seeing it any other way. Learning to fight the bias involves acknowledging your qualities and talents, rather than discounting them. "I like drawing. I was good at it even in Lower KG." "I have always been a good listener." Remember prejudices can be changed, but they are apt to re-emerge in times of stress.

Surround yourself with Positive and Supportive People

Mix with people who will build up your confidence and self-esteem. Make friends with those who are positive, enthusiastic and success oriented. Spend your time with people who make you feel good. It will be a great idea to derive inspiration from your role models. Negative people will constantly put you down and your self-esteem is diminished. Eleanor Roosevelt very rightly said, "Nobody can make me inferior without my permission." Do you agree with Eleanor?

Feel Good

Stop making excuses for not achieving your goals, ambition and success. Here are some of the excuses which you should always avoid.

- I am not intelligent.
- I am too proud.
- I am not made that way.
- If only I was handsome.
- I am always unlucky.

Get Involved

You should get involved in work and activities that inspire you. Spend leisure time on hobbies and activities you find stimulating. It is great to relax and remain cheerful.

Don't Fear Mistakes

Every mistake is an experience from which you can gain information to achieve success in the future. Mistakes are only unsatisfactory results, then why to fear them?

Respect your own Needs and Wants

If you respect your own needs and wants, it will increase your sense of self worth and well-being. Further, solve problems and don't complain about them. You need to have an attitude of openness and should be curious about new facts, ideas, experiences and new possibilities in life.

Accept Positive Feedback

When you turn to the outside world for affirmations, make sure you accept the bad feedback as quickly as you accept the good one. Positive feedback matters, because it helps us to confirm that we're on the right track.

Take Action

When you take action, irrespective of its result, you feel better. Learn to move forward and be free of anxiety and fear. Be flexible when responding to challenges and earn trust of others by honouring the commitments you make to them.

Convey a Positive Image

You need to convey an image of yourself as one who is

positive and has a high self-esteem. This can be achieved. You must dress up well and move smartly with a high sense of pride.

Keep a Record

It's a good idea to keep a record of every successful experience you have, both in your studies and personal life. This information can be stored in a scrap book or even on your computer along with photos and letters. Whenever you feel low, refer to this record and it will help you to re-establish a self belief. Further, visualisation of successful events of the past can make you cheerful and make you feel great.

Do you know that the words you use have a tremendous effect on your being great? Let me illustrate this by an interesting story. Kamni's mother took her to a grooming school. Her mother soil that Kamni was a very difficult and unusual child, who would need special attention. She told the trainer, "Look at my daughter, she is ugly and awful. What can you do for her?" Kamni's training was tough going at first. Kamni's thoughts about herself mirrored her mother's views. To live up to her mother's expectations, she was rebellious, apathetic and reluctant to listen or participate, but she wanted to improve. As she improved, she stood taller and expressed herself more clearly.

Soon, Kamni's self perception changed. She discovered how very attractive she was. She learned how to carry herself with pride, look people into their eyes and share her inner and outer beauty with them. She no longer thought about herself in the way her mother had trained her. Her confidence soared. At the end of the four weeks training, she asked her mother to let her continue in professional group classes of commercial acting and photography. By this time, her mother was willing to let her join the group courses and her progress advanced even more rapidly. Kamni learned that she was not "awful" and she enjoyed being in front of the camera that proved to her, she was not "ugly." This true story demonstrates the power of words over thinking and behaviour and its effect on self-worth of a human being.

In a nutshell, never take things too seriously or personally. Always take up challenges and act according to your values. To build greatness, don't compare yourself with others, bury the prejudice, feed good and respect your needs and wants. Get involved and don't fear mistakes. People will say, "you are great."

9

Confidence Leads to Success

"Whether you think you can or you think you can't, you're right."
—Henry Ford

Sachin Tendulkar is one of the greatest cricketer ever born on our planet. He is a role model not only to the youth but also to the people of other ages who admire him. He is considered a genius batsman, "MASTER BLASTER". Even then, he is down to earth. What makes him so great? I guess it's his discipline, focus, commitment and deep passion for the game. He has lots of confidence. All of us agree to that.

Do you know that confidence is a belief in you that says you can manage anything? Many a time, you are afraid to try new things because you feel you may fail and that will not look good. However, trying is what is most important. If you do not try, you have already failed. So you have nothing to lose by trying. By not trying, you do not even give yourself a chance to succeed. Having confidence enables you to take up new challenges and trust yourself in difficult situations. The confidence spectrum can be represented by:

Supreme confidence
(Confidence + belief)
Example: I'll win.

Confidence
(Natural capability)
Example: I should win.

Arrogance
(Supreme confidence + assumption)
Example: I always win.

How Confident Are You?

To assess your current state of confidence, for each of the 10 statements below, rate yourself on a scale of 1–5 (where 1 means you agree strongly with the statement and 5 means you disagree strongly with it).

- I am not smart.
- I am scared of saying no to others.
- I feel the need to be accepted by agreeing with everyone.
- I often think I am not good enough.
- I don't forgive myself for my mistakes.
- I often compare myself unfavourably with others.
- I do not feel confident in social situations.
- I am frightened with the idea of achieving success.

- I find it difficult to make decisions.
- I do not believe in my self.

Your Score

Under 15:	Lack of confidence is really holding you back.
16–35 :	You need to work on your confidence.
Over 36	You are well on your way to having the confidence.

How does a Juggler's kid learn Confidence?

How does a Juggler's kid who walks on the rope, learn to perform with confidence? It is acquired by coaching, relentless practice and an assurance of safety. Assurance can come from two sources, from others and from within.

How did you learn your Confidence?

From the time of birth, you receive messages from the outside world which build up or drain your confidence. Then there are certain other factors like school, society and environment which affect the confidence. Initially, it is just parental influence. The child is encouraged to walk and talk. Parents encourage the child and help him to grow. By the time the child is ready to go to school, things start changing and a number of restrictions are placed on him, "Don't do this; this is not right", and so on. Further, some parents neglect the child while some put unnecessary pressure on him to perform. Consequently, the child begins to lose confidence. There is no gain saying that parents play an important role in developing the confidence base of the child as well as his self-image.

Let us take a look at what knocks down confidence and self-esteem at this stage.

- Being ridiculed or humiliated.
- Being compared with someone, "your brother is better than you."
- Being told, "You are not intelligent."
- When feelings of the child are ignored.

Subsequently, school and society have a significant role to play. Apart from parents a child is influenced by relationships he develops with other people. During this period, how a child is treated and cared for has a great effect on his confidence. Then, there are environmental and other factors, which decide the confidence level. The place in society and external events also play their part.

The Confidence Plan

You need to have a confidence plan to succeed in life. The confidence plan consists of nine steps.

Step 1: Know Yourself

You should identify the areas you need to develop and skills you need to learn. Once you know that, it will make you feel confident.

Step 2: Be Action Oriented

Make a list of actions you need to take to achieve your aim. You must concentrate on actions which will improve your confidence level. Gradually move on to actions which require greater effort. To gain confidence, be proactive, i.e., gaining control by taking initiative.

Step 3: Learn to Focus

It is a known fact that whatever you focus on, it grows and develops. You need to look your strengths and weaknesses. Try to improve upon your areas of strength and natural abilities. Rosalyn Carter says, *"you got to have confidence in your ability and then be tough enough to follow through"*. You could develop your talents and skills, improve your memory, your friendly nature and so on. Learn to keep the bigger picture in mind and do not let your efforts be wasted on trivial matters.

Step 4: Control Fear

Life has ups and downs, pleasures and sorrows, success and failures. The best way to overcome fear is to keep doing the thing you fear to do. You should try to identify the causes of fear and trigger points so that you can gradually eliminate them. Let go off the past and live in the present.

Step 5: Have Good Relationships

Man is a social animal and has to live with others. Remember, your confidence is affected by the company you keep. So, you must keep away from moaners, crushers and critics. You must spend time with people who value you, and you feel good in their company.

Step 6: Act Confident

If you act with confidence you will find that people will react to you positively. Try saying to yourself, "I am respected and I'm a nice person". When you have such thoughts in your mind, you will surely notice the change in your outlook.

Further, you need to have a pleasant appearance, so dress up smartly and look cheerful. A smile on the face adds to your confidence.

Step 7: Have Positive Thoughts

Confidence comes from within and is built on what and how you think. When you think positively about yourself, it will raise your confidence level. Here is a short list of positive thoughts:

- It's a great day.
- I am energetic and happy.
- I love my family and friends. I am happy at school.
- Life is so interesting.
- This will also pass, so why to worry.

Step 8: Empowering words

Words can be empowering. We can reach a new level of living, if we feed ourselves with empowering words and continue saying them until they become a habit. Use empowering words like, ***'I can; I want to; I must; I love to, etc.'***

Step 9: Protect your confidence level

Look at the table below, to know who are the confidence Robbers and who are Boosters.

Confidence Robbers	*Confidence Boosters*
Cognitive	
• Selective perception	• Focus on the good as well as the bad
• Selective memory	• Remember the good as well as the bad
• Unrealistic comparisons	• Create a different future
Self-awareness	
• Not aware of own worth	• Keep generating your personal portfolio
• Lack of belief in self	• Know your worth
• Reliance on the external	• Be self-reliant for acknowledgement
Fear	
• Failure	• Plan for worst case scenario
• Fear of making mistakes	• Use the handling mistakes process
Letting yourself down	
• Lack of responsibility	• Accept the consequences of your actions
• Lack of commitment	• Remember setbacks are temporary

In a nutshell, confidence can act as a springboard for success in your personal and professional life. When you are confident, life seems exciting and you are more likely to persist so that you can achieve the desired goals. There are various factors which influence the level of confidence. Initially there is parental influence and subsequently it is the school and society which have a significant role to play. To succeed in life you must prepare and follow the nine steps of a confidence plan.

10

Translate Dreams into Reality

"A journey of a thousand miles must begin with a single step."

—Lao Tzu

Who does not know Professor Hawking? He is a true genius. He has been confined to the chair for over 30 years. He is unable to talk or move his hands and legs. Hawking can only make tiny facial expressions using the muscles around his eyes, eye-brows, cheek and mouth. He suffers from motor neuron disease which does not affect the brain or the senses. He has a team of ten nurses to attend him in three shifts. He is spoonfed. A man who has been confined to a wheel chair, has written the famous book, 'A Brief History of Time', in which he explains the origin of the universe. The book has been translated into 65 languages and has become one of the biggest selling non-fiction books of all times. Don't you think that it requires superhuman courage to develop this kind of mental strength? During 2008, Prof. Hawking volunteered to fly in the zero gravity zone. He stated, "I have wanted to fly in space all my life", and added, "For someone

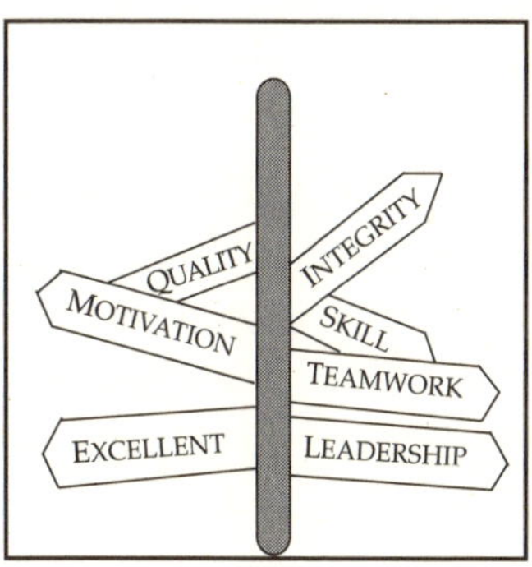

like me whose muscles don't work very well, it will be a bliss to be weightless". There is no other way to describe the motivational level of Hawking; he deserves a twentyone gun salute.

What is motivation? Well, motivation is the ability to satisfy a need, desire, expectation or goal without being influenced to do so by another person. It is the driving force which initiates and directs behaviour, based on three specific aspects such as the arousal of behavior, the direction of behaviour and persistence of behaviour. We can also say that it is a form of self-encouragement. A person with high level of motivation takes initiative. He is a self-starter and is always positively proactive in whatever he does. He is cool, calm and composed.

If you want to excel in life, motivation is essential. Self-motivation comes from building confidence in your own skills and abilities, recognizing your self-worth and valuing your experiences.

Motivation is the power that translates our dreams into reality. Whatever we do is primarily based on the intensity of motivation. Martin Luther King believed, *"If a man hasn't discovered something that he will die for, he isn't fit to live."* There are three main things that motivate people; what they want to achieve, own and influence.

Ways of staying Self-motivated

Self-motivation does fluctuate up and down. This could be due to unpleasant remarks or unwarranted actions of other people. In addition, we are also equally responsible for fluctuations in our level of motivation. Therefore, there is an urgent need to learn the ways of staying self motivated. Get to know what motivates you and what does not.

To keep the spark of self motivation, you should keep going and take action. Don't forget that people will judge you by your actions and not by your intentions. Get out of your comfort zone and learn to get into unfamiliar surroundings to explore better opportunities. Instead of cribbing over what you don't have, concentrate on what you have and want to achieve. Affirm daily that you can achieve what you want to and no obstacle can stop you. Napoleon Hill said, *"Life's battles don't always go to the stronger or faster man. But sooner or later the man who wins, is the man who thinks he can."*

Be persistent and feel enthusiastic of whatever, you want to achieve. The great inventions of Thomas A Edison were fruits of his persistence. He said, *"Genius is 1% inspiration and 99% perspiration.... I never did anything worth by accident nor did any of my inventions come by accident, they came by hard work."*

Don't let an unwelcome result turn into a semipermanent set-back. Learn what is to be learnt from the experience and then let it go. It is not until you do that you will find the energy and motivation to start moving forward again. Alexander Graham Bell, the inventor of telephone, had faced many failures before he could make an instrument that worked. About his failed experiments, he said, *"When one door closes another opens, but we often look so long and so regretfully on the closed door that we do not see the one which has opened for us."*

Let me explain this through an interesting story. One day, two frogs were enjoying the day in the barn when they accidentally fell into the farmer's bucket of cream, and they couldn't get out. The two frogs kept swimming around to save themselves from drowning. Every once in a while they tried to climb out, but this was becoming very tiring. One frog kept saying, "This is useless, we should just give up." But the other frog just ignored the comment and kept swimming. Finally, the pessimistic frog gave up and drowned. The other frog became sad at the loss of his friend, but he didn't give up. He kept swimming. Finally, the cream turned into butter and the frog simply climbed out. This story shows that even if we stumble and others try to discourage us, we should not give up. We can overcome the obstacles with courage and persistence.

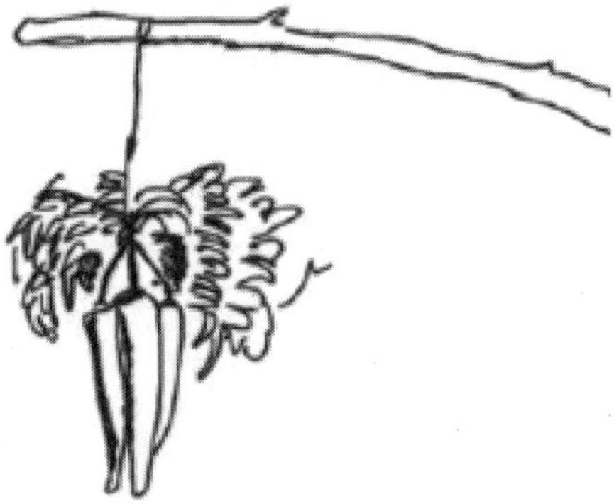

Outdated Method of Motivation

Assessment: Level of Motivation

Given below are ten statements. Answer each statement with either. Always or Sometimes or Never.

- I work to satisfy my needs and expectations.
- I am more relaxed when going gets tough.
- I believe in persistence and never resist change.
- I read self-development books.
- I am full of energy throughout the day.

- I believe in working hard to achieve my goals.
- I believe in myself.
- I never try to stay in the comfort zone.
- Criticism does not demotivate me.
- Failures and set backs do not put me down.

Your Score. If your answer to 8 to 10 statements is **Always,** your level of motivation is high.

If your answer to less than 5 statements is **Always,** you need to work on your motivation.

What matters most is how you see yourself

Saina Nehwal is a super hero in the game of badminton. Presently, she is ranked number 2 in the world. Her rise has been nothing short of meteoric. Her coach explains, "Saina has a very positive approach towards life. She is clear about what she wants to achieve. She is extremely hard working and honest about her training. She trains herself for six hours a day. Saina is well disciplined and mentally strong. These qualities are vital for success." Isn't Saina extremely motivated and genius in the sports field? There is no doubt about it.

How to Stay Motivated the whole day?

It's not easy to always stay motivated for the whole day. There are times when challenges and problems strike us and make us feel bad. Well, don't let this happen. Remain motivated and energized throughout the day. Given below are some tips, to stay motivated the whole day:

Rise Early

For some people rising early is a kind of magic. It makes them feel more enthusiastic and energized throughout the day. Maybe, it's because by rising early they can start the day fresh without having to rush on everything. It gives them more time to prepare themselves mentally and physically to face the day.

Dress up Well

Have you ever noticed that how your dressing up can affect your feeling? Some dresses make you feel better, whereas some particular dress can make you feel uncomfortable.

Energize yourself

Sometimes, the biggest problem is the lack of energy. To energize yourself, listen to music, have energy drinks, do deep breathing exercises, meditation, etc. You should use the leisure time in a hobby or any activity which you enjoy.

Pick "Quote of the Day"

Pick your favourite quote in the morning and keep it in mind throughout the day. Of course, the quote should be something that motivates and inspires you. Speak out the quote to yourself throughout the day, especially when you think that you need extra motivation. This way, it will be easier to get rid of negative thoughts because you always have something positive to say to yourself. Have you ever paid attention to the blockboard, where Quote of the Day is written.

Find the Positive Side of everything

One main cause for losing motivation is thinking negative about some events which are happening to you. Every time you think negatively about something, you actually lose a part of your energy. Do it for the whole day and you will feel very exhausted and even intimidated by the end of the day. So look for the positive side of everything.

Focus on Giving

Contributing to others is always motivating. It works for me. I don't know why, but maybe it's because by doing so, I focus less on my own problems. It doesn't mean that I run away from the problems, it just means that the problems seem less daunting and intimidating. Because I'm not just thinking about myself. Further, there is something about giving that gives you extra happiness. Brighten someone else's life and your life will also be brightened.

Decide to be a Winner

It is your decision that makes the difference between winning and losing. Nothing can make you lose, if you don't allow it to do so. Decide to be a winner. If you decide to be a winner then you will be tough and brave while facing all challenges throughout the day. You will not let problems overcome you. Instead, you will step in and conquer those problems. You will be the winner, who can resist you?

In a nutshell, motivation is the ability to satisfy needs, desires, expectations or goals without being influenced to do so by another person. Motivation means fulfilling needs, having good relationships and influences over people. Persistence is the key to success. Failures must be seen as stepping-stones to success. Learn from experience and move on. To gain momentum in motivation, it is better to start simple and thereafter move towards difficult tasks.

11

Understand the Thinking System

*"A man is but a product of his thoughts,
What he thinks, that he becomes."*
—***Mahatma Gandhi***

One of the greatest discoveries of human mind is that we are products of our own thinking. Once you master the way of thinking, you can master your destiny. There is a magnetic force generated within you, which draws you to whatever your mind centres upon. As your mind power develops, so does this magnetic force and you start attracting conditions and people who promote success. The mind has two levels, conscious and sub-conscious. The conscious mind is the thinking mind that reasons, debates and analyzes. On the other hand, sub-conscious is the memory store for all the information received from the conscious mind. It does not have the ability to differentiate between positive or negative information, true or false, because it accepts the information as a fact. Usually nothing is received by the sub-conscious mind that has not been processed by the conscious mind for a length of time. It is believed that sub-conscious mind controls the behavior and heavily influences what materializes in our life. So, we need to understand the thinking system so that we can improve ourselves and achieve success.

Five Step Thinking System

Step	
Beliefs and values ⇩	Are generated from influences around you
Thoughts ⇩	How you interact with others and yourself
Emotions ⇩	Beliefs, values, thoughts and expectations drive your emotions
Behaviour ⇩	Emotions and thoughts directly affect your behaviour
Action	Means what you do

Beliefs and Values

Have you ever wondered as to how you have learnt your beliefs and values? Do they have an impact on your life? Beliefs and values are ways of thinking and behaving that are literally learnt from parents, teachers and role models. They are your acceptance of a set of values in social and moral guidelines. Further, beliefs shape opinions and assumptions about situations and people. It is seen that most of the day-to-day conditioning while growing up consists of **'don'ts'**. This gives rise to self limiting beliefs which cause hindrance to your success. Some of the self limiting beliefs could be,

"Don't speak, know your place", "Don't try to be clever", "Don't bite more than you can chew", etc. You must get rid of your limiting beliefs. Believe in yourself and believe that you can succeed. When you believe something can be done, your mind will find ways to do it.

Thoughts

Beliefs and values influence thoughts and expectations of life. It also influences your interaction with yourself, others and the world at large. It is wisely said, "A thought can ruin you, but a thought can also make you". Positive thought has the power to change one's attitude, well-being and destiny. Every action begins with a thought. Constructive thoughts lead to constructive actions, foolish thoughts to foolish actions, destructive thoughts to destructive actions. Most human beings are severely limited by their thinking. When you become aware of the effects your thoughts can have on your life, you become very conscious of what you're thinking. You start taking control of your thoughts. How you manage your thoughts is under your control. Therefore, by choosing to think positively, you can choose positive goals, positive words, and positive actions, thereby creating positive conditions in your life.

Here are some affirmations that may appeal to you and will help to keep negative thoughts away from your mind.

- Every day I must keep my thoughts positive.
- I must always maintain a healthy body and mind.
- I am happy and healthy.
- I only think about and visualize what I want to happen.

- I have balance and harmony in my life.
- I can achieve whatever I set in my mind.
- I can achieve anything I want.
- I will persist until I succeed.
- I am in a radiant and dynamic health.
- I believe in myself.
- I like myself.
- I am cool, calm and in control.
- I am successful in everything I do.

Positive phrases empower people and let them take control of what to believe. "I think, I will," is probably the most recognizable positive phrase today. First of all, the act of saying a positive thinking phrase to yourself may distract you from the daunting task at hand and enable you to just react. By saying "I think, I can" to yourself and taking step to overcome your problem, you will take your mind off the impossibility of the task and you will be able to do it.

Positive phrases also help you by strengthening your belief. If you say a positive phrase enough number of times, you may be able to stir up your belief and really achieve your goal. By repeating a positive phrase, we trigger a response within ourselves that helps us to forget everything and strengthen our will. A positive phrase will help us believe and belief is a very powerful it.

Let me tell you an important secret of the mind. Your mind always gravitates towards what you think about the most. If you think of success most of the time, your mind will program it in the sub-conscious mind. It will prompt you to do things so that your want/desire is fulfilled.

Another secret is that your mind works on pictures. When you say to yourself, 'I don't want to forget my pen,' you form a picture of forgetting. Since the mind works on that picture, the result is you forget your pen. Instead, if you tell yourself,' I want to remember my pen,' you will form a mental picture of remembering, and you will be in a far better position to remember.

There is one more secret of the mind. Are you keen to know? Of course you are. That's why you are reading this book. The secret of your mind is that it cannot and will not work on the reverse of an idea. To illustrate, when you tell a child, 'George, don't break the vase', you are heading for trouble, because the brain does not picture the word don't, but picturizes break. What do you learn from this secret? Simple! Think and say positive words to yourself and to others.

Somebody has so beautifully said,

> *"Watch your thoughts, they become your words.*
> *Watch your words, they become your actions.*
> *Watch your actions, they become your habit.*
> *Watch your habits, they become your character.*
> *Watch your character, it becomes your destiny."*

Emotions

Emotions, which we understand as feelings, are caused by thoughts. When you are happy, cheerful, excited, valued by people, you experience positive feelings. On the contrary, negative feelings are experienced when you are angry, depressed or upset. Feelings guide you where you want to go and are like a compass. They connect you to others and also show how distinct you are when compared to other people. When you do not feel well, you may visualize something that will calm you down, it could be a waterfall, calm sea or walking in a beautiful airy park. This will help you to shift your mind from unpleasant feeling to calmness. You could also chant a mantra. Remember, never get emotionally charged as there are certain things you can control and some others which you cannot control; hence, pay attention to the things you can control.

Behaviour

The feeling of a man is reflected on his behaviour. Once a behaviour is repeated a number of times it automatically becomes a habit. Habits are the first requisite to the formation of a character of a person. Habits are either termed as good or as bad.

- **Good Habits.** They help us to advance in life and lead a healthy life. One must inculcate good habits like taking exercises regularly, keeping the body clean and healthy. Cultivate the habit of mixing with people, which will lead you to understand them.
- **Bad Habits.** Bad habits destroy a person's character. They also affect his/her performance. They close so many doors for you. If you are a drunkard you can't visit a place of worship as people do not appreciate someone in that state. If you are a compulsive liar, people stop trusting you. The essence of bad habits springs from lack of self-control.

Actions

Your thoughts become your actions and your actions create the circumstances in your life. You are responsible for everything that happens to you in your life. This is simply based on 'As you sow so you reap'. It can also be called the law of motion and emotion. Every thought that we send out into the universe comes back to us with an accumulated energy of its own kind. When negative thoughts are send out of our minds, they come back to us with a doubled forced negative energy and give us lot of pain and unhappiness. Positive thoughts, on the other hand, bring in positive energy and energize us, establishing in the peace process and harmony in our consciousness. Our actions too yield the same results. Thus, through our actions and thoughts we are constantly creating our own realities. Taking action in life is important. To achieve success, you got to wake up and take required actions.

Now you know

- The thinking system includes beliefs and values, thoughts, emotions, behaviour and actions. Every action begins with a thought. Therefore, choose to think positively. You are the master of your destiny. Through thoughts and actions, you are constantly creating your own realities.
- Don't get emotionally charged as there are things you can control and things which you may not be able to control. Suppressing negative feelings can lead to all sorts of troubles like low self-image, stress, anger, etc. Try to keep your negative emotions under check.

- Good habits will help you to advance in life. Always be nice to people and earn their trust. If you want success in life, then get rid of your bad habits.

12

To Achieve Greatness, Get Rid of your Limiting Beliefs

"There is only one cause of unhappiness; the false beliefs you have in your mind, beliefs so widespread, so commonly held, that it never occurs to you to question them."

—Anthony de Mello

Have you ever thought how limiting beliefs can stop you from achieving greatness? It is said that when an elephant is young it is tied to a huge post which is much bigger than necessary to keep the animal from breaking free. The elephant tries day after day to break free and finally gives up. The elephant is, in this way, conditioned to believe that it cannot escape. As it grows, the post it is tied to becomes no match as compared to the elephant's mighty strength. However, because of its conditioning, it doesn't even try to break free.

Since our birth, we also, are conditioned that form beliefs within us. Many of these beliefs are LIMITING! Let's say you have come from a family with below average income. You have seen your father and mother struggling from pay cheque to pay cheque to make both ends meet. Over a period of time, you may have formed a belief that everyone in your family has to live in this way because no one in your family has ever become rich.

Here is an inspirational story of a company which brings out that we should accept changes in life and go beyond our limiting beliefs. One day all the employees of a very unusual company reached their office to see a big sign on the main door which said, "The person who has been hindering your growth in this company passed away yesterday. We invite you to join the funeral that has been prepared in the gym." In the beginning, they all were sad for the death of one of their colleagues, but after a while they started getting curious to know who was that person who hindered the growth of their colleagues and the company itself? The excitement in the gym was such that security agents were ordered to control the crowd within the room. As more and more people reached hear the coffin, the excitement there heated up. Everyone wondered, 'Who is this person, who was hindering my progress?' One by one the intrigued employees got closer to the coffin, and when they looked inside it, they suddenly became speechless. They all ended up shocked and in silence, as if someone had touched the deepest part of their soul. There was a mirror inside the coffin; everyone who looked inside it saw themselves! There was also a sign next to the mirror that said, "there is only one person who is capable of setting limits to your growth and it is you." Your life does not change when your boss changes, when your friends change, when your parents change, when your husband or wife changes, when your company changes, when your location changes, when your money changes, when your status changes. Your life changes when you change, when you go beyond your limiting beliefs.

Building Beliefs

It is like learning to drive. When you first learnt to drive a car, you were aware of all thoughts and actions you needed to take to pass the test. As driving became a habit, you now no longer pay conscious attention to 'how to' drive. Driving has become automatic. In a similar way, the habits resulting from your belief systems affect the way you think, learn and communicate and yet you can be totally unaware of these silent forces at work.

Answer YES or NO to following statements:

- You must remind yourself that you are the "best."
- One must get rid of the limiting beliefs.
- Successful people are just ordinary people who have developed belief in themselves and their doings.
- Think big and remember that big ideas and plans are generally easier to achieve than you initially think.
- People who reach the top rungs in business management, selling, writing or any other pursuit, get there by following a plan for self-development and growth.
- Perception forms the bases of all our beliefs and actions.

In case, your answer is "NO" to more than two of the above statements, you need to work on your limiting beliefs.

Common Limiting Beliefs

Everyone has limiting beliefs hidden inside them. Successful people over-come limiting beliefs and achieve their goals. Given below are some of the most common limiting beliefs.

You could be harbouring one of them.

Limiting Beliefs:	*Change your Beliefs to:*
1. I can't do it.	I can do it.
2. I am not good enough.	I am good enough.
3. I don't deserve.	I deserve the best.
4. I am not worthy.	I am worthy.
5. I am not lucky.	I'm lucky.
6. It is too late for me.	It is never too late.
7. Money is evil.	Money is good.
8. I am not smart/slim/clever.	I am smart/slim/clever.
9. I will fail.	I will pass.
10. People are selfish.	People are good.

You must make a list of beliefs which are holding you back. These are beliefs which are not serving you well and also, not helping you to take adult decisions. Look at the list and do the following:

- Change your belief system instantly and when you master changes, tick them off from your list.
- Then look at those beliefs which are harder to change. Think of how you are going to get rid of these beliefs and lay down a time period.
- Finally, you may come to a belief which is very difficult to change and will require a lot of effort. You must take action to get rid of it in a systematic manner.

I am reminded of a monk who had grand ideas to change the world. He wrote in the 12th century:

When I was a young man, I wanted to change the world. I found it was difficult to change the world, so I tried to change my nation.

When I found I couldn't change the nation, I began to focus on my town. I couldn't change the town and as an elderly man, I tried to change my family.

Now, as an old man, I realize the only thing I can change is myself; and suddenly I realize that if long ago I had changed myself, I could have made an impact on my family. My family and I could have made an impact on our town. Their impact could have changed the nation and I could indeed have changed the world.

In a nutshell, one must get rid of self limiting beliefs. Always think of success and say 'I can', 'I can do it', 'I am the best' and so on.

The biggest obstacles to creating a wonderful life
Are self limiting beliefs.
A self limiting belief is an idea
You have that you're limited in some way,
In terms of time, talent, intelligence,
Money, ability or opportunity.

—Brian Tracy

Don't ever fear belief, rather have the courage to embrace positive beliefs and get on with your life.

—Scott Moore

When you believe, 'i can do it',
The 'how to do it', develops.

—David Schwartz

13

Live Your Life with Values

*"It's not hard to make decisions
When you know what your values are."*

—Roy Disney

A mountaineering team had prepared themselves for three years to take part in a competitive climb. After leaving their second camp, they came across a seriously injured climber. Those were the days when there were no cell phones. One of the members of the team, decided to drop out of the climb and bring down the injured person. The other members pleaded with him not to do so. But he had a strong value system in which helping others was on top of the list. When asked why he did this, his response was, "If I would have let that young man die, no matter what success I would have achieved, I could not have lived with that thought for the rest of my life." So, we can say that values determine our preferences, priorities and actions.

You learn certain values from your experience, upbringing and culture, education system and working life. Your value system indicates what is important to you and helps in making decisions more easily. In addition, values help in dealing with difficult people and situations. You must identify values, which are meaningful to you and set priorities to achieve these values. A way to determine your own values can be by thinking about some people, for example, if you don't like arrogant people, you value humbleness. At times people recognize the value after they go through a crisis or painful experience. For example, when do most people recognize the value of good health? It's obvious; when they fall sick.

To be a success, you must learn to live with your values and at no stage compromise with them. I believe, if you have your principles and values in place and use them correctly, you'll have a lot of peace in life. Further, values like gratitude and apology are emotional yardsticks of a human character. Therefore, values must be practised with full sincerity to derive total benefit from them. You should have clear core values and live by them to avoid painful inner conflicts. Life will change for you when you take actions based on your value systems.

Choose the values that are most important to you, the values you believe in and that define your character. Then live them visibly every day at work and at home. Living with your values is one of the most powerful tools available to you. It will help you to be the person you want to be, to help you accomplish your goals and dreams, and lead and influence others. Don't waste your best opportunity.

Have you ever wondered what your values are? Write down ten values in order of priority which you consider important. Given below are some universal values to help you choose:

Enthusiasm	Fun/Joy	People	Integrity
Adventure	Healthy	Power	Courage
Ambition	Honest	Recognition	Dedication
Faithful	Humorous	Religion	Bliss
Creativity	Humble	Independence	Respect
Challenge	Security	Family	Success
Keeping promises	Freedom	Learning	Travel
Friendship	Love	Gratitude	Money
Trust			

Try to imbibe the 10 values selected by you, in your day-to-day life. Let's say you have selected humour. In such a situation, you should learn new jokes and alway try to remain happy. Be with people who are filled with energy. Learn to smile at yourself. Finally, the values you choose must allow you to achieve your ultimate goal in life. In case a value is not contributing towards your goal, then the value needs to be changed. Once you are clear about your values, there is a greater chance to notice how your life needs to change.

How we respond to a situation depends on how strongly we wish to uphold our personal value system. These values are tested a number of times. In the case of the mountaineer, he paid the price of not reaching the summit. He was prepared to forego the successes that could have followed. He let all that go for saving a life.

Sachin Tendulkar, 'The Master Blaster' who is the world's greatest cricketer, in an interview, said, *"My focus is always on what I am trying to achieve. Not on what I have already achieved"*. A true mark of a champion! He talks of his two children and states that he always keeps a balance between pampering and discipline *"Just because I can afford to give them whatever they want in the world, doesn't mean that I have to do so. I always talk to them about how every successful person has to work hard and be disciplined."* Well! Sachin, that's a great value you have taught to your children.

In a nutshell, value system indicates what is important and it helps in making sound decisions. Make a list of values and gradually imbibe them in your day-to-day life.

> *Men of genius are admired,*
> *Men of wealth are envied,*
> *Men of power are feared,*
> *But only men of character are trusted.*
>
> ***—Alfred Adler***

14

Know the Power of Positive Thinking and Positive Attitude

A positive attitude brings strength, energy and initiative.
—Remez Sasson

Once a man asked a wise man, who was sitting at the main gate of a city, "I would like to live in your city. What kind of people does it have?" The wise man replied, "What kind of people are there in the city you have come from?" To this the man replied, "Oh, they are not very nice. They lie, cheat and steal. That's why I want to move out". The wise man replied, "It's the same way here. If I were you, I'd keep looking". A short time later another man came up and asked about the people in the city. The wise man asked the man about his own city. The second man replied, "They're wonderful, they always help each other. They are truthful and industrious. I just thought I'd like to see other parts of the world." The wise man in his wisdom replied, "It's the same way here. Why don't you go into the city? You'll find it just as you imagine it should be." Why did

the wise man invite the second man to enter the city? This story makes it clear that when we move, we carry our attitude and way of thinking with us. You will be welcomes only if your attitude and thinking are positive.

Effects of Positive Thinking?

To achieve success, you need to have positive thoughts and expectations. Positive thoughts have definite effect on your speech or words taht you say. Also, the reality we experience is a sum total of our thoughts. Therefore, tell positive things to the mind. Positive thinking must also be focused on a positive belief system. Positive results will come when you refrain from your negative thoughts.

Power of Words?

Words influence our perception about the world. Right words make us feel positive and wrong words make us feel negative. If we know this, then why don't we use positive words to ourselves and to others. Words we use are powerful and can work wonders or can lead towards doom. Let me explain what happened at one of the seminars. A speaker was explaining about the power of positive thinking and the power of words. One member from the audience raised his hand and said, "Only saying good fortune, good fortune, good fortune, to myself will not make me feel better. Nor if I will say bad luck, bad luck, bad luck, it will make me feel worse. They're only words and, by they have no power." The speaker replied, "You, son of a..." The member of the audience was stunned, his face became red. He was about to reply back when the speaker raised his hand and said,"Please excuse me. I didn't mean to upset you. Please accept my most sincere apologies." The member of the audience calmed down. Some people in the hall murmured; others shuffled their feet. The speaker resumed, "There's the reply to the question you asked me. A few words made you very angry. The others calmed you down."

You should be confident and have positive outlook towards life. Be enthusiastic, enterprizing and be proactive. Try to see the positive hidden in every negative experience. How you see a particular event depends upon your perception, therefore, react to situations in a positive manner and avoid self-imposed limitations on yourself. Avoid feelings of resentment, ill-will, jealousy, hatred, etc.

Begin your day with a positive thought in mind. Interact with constructive people and help out those who you can help you to become more positive. Accept others as they are, don't judge or blame others without going into the facts. Concentrate on what others have done for you and not on what they have npt. Your aim should be to build bridges and not walls.

Always give a positive impression. Your appearance tells a lot about your attitude. Try to realize how you sit, stand or walk. Also, have a positive body language and a vibrant personality with an open state of mind. You should appear to be in complete harmony from within.

Take time out to acknowledge personal achievements and celebrate success. Get rid of negative pattern in life. Be assertive and control anxiety by filtering out irrational thoughts and beliefs. Interrupt your negative thoughts and replace them with positive ones. Become more aware of your emotions.

In the game of Tambola, when the announcer has number 6 in his hand, he calls, "When in a fix, cut out six." Well, in life you may have to deal with situations where you can't decide and find yourself in a fix. The best way is to Ask Yourself.

Situation	*Ask Yourself*
When I worry	Will the successful person I know be disturbed about this?
An idea	What will the important person do, if he had this idea?
My appearance	Do I look like someone who has self-respect?
My language	Is my language like the successful people?
What I read	Will an important person read this?
Conversation	Is this something successful people will discuss?
When I lose my temper	Will an important person get mad at what I'm mad at?
My jokes	Is this the kind of joke an important person will tell?
My job	How does an important person like what I do?

Eliminate Negativity

Negative thinking destroys relationships, achievement and happiness. It has an inverse effect on emotions, both, physical and mental. Avoid common phrases which people often say to themselves like "I know I can't", "I am too old", or "I am not capable". To eliminate negativity, always think before you say something to somebody. It should have a positive effect and in no way demoralize or demotivate anyone. This is equally true about what you say to yourself. Avoid negative situations at home and at place of work. Try to understand other's point of view and do not over-react. Get out of the habit of negative thinking. It will take time to quit this habit but give it a try, it is well worth trying.

Positive Attitude

What is Attitude? Attitude is the sum total of a person's beliefs, assumptions, expectations and values.

Beliefs + Assumptions + Expectations + Values = Attitude

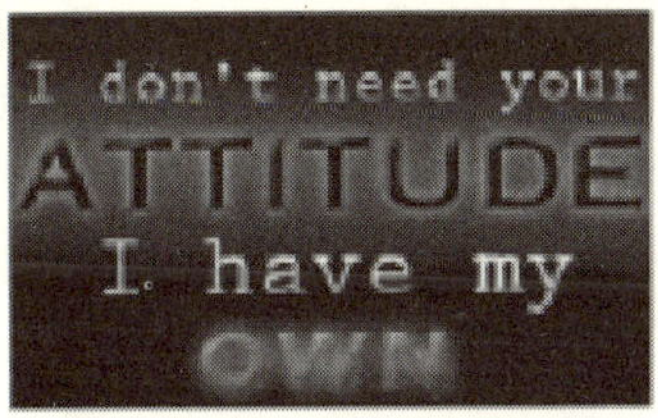

Attitude is defined as 'the way a person feels, thinks and behaves towards a particular issue'. How we think reflects through the way we act. Attitudes are the mirrors of mind. They reflect thinking. We read the attitude through expressions, voice and tones. Behavioural scientists have defined it as the 'mental box' which helps to show a person, a particular situation in a specific frame of mind. In life, winner is one who has positive attitude, self belief and the determination to succeed. A positive thinker does not see set backs as stumbling blocks, rather he considers them as stepping stones.

Attitude is a state of mind and positive attitude manifests in progressive, creative and constructive thinking. It brings optimism in life and expectation of success. It also helps in believing in self, and in displaying self-esteem and self-confidence. Behaviour derives from attitude. So you can change your behaviour by changing your attitude. Attitude makes the difference. Students with the

right attitude constitute A grade, and right attitude pave the way to a really happy life. Attitude plays a part virtually in every phase of life. A vision to succeed and hard work is an unbeatable positive combination. You can find two ways to look at everything virtually. A pessimist looks for difficulty in every opportunity, whereas an optimistic looks for opportunity in every difficulty. There is an old saying, *"Two men looked out of the window, one saw mud, and the other saw stars."*

Your life today is the result of your attitude and choices in the past. Your life tomorrow will be the result of your attitudes and choices of today. Let me explain what an attitude is, with the help of a story. Sheila felt that she was on the fast track. She had a relentless focus on her career and eschewed all activities that did not help her to move upward. She did not attend the Fridaynight parties unless she knew that her boss or his boss would be there. Then she became the life of the party. She did not like volunteering, but chose to do so at the same disadvantaged-Youth Centre where the general manager went. She made sure she was there on the same days. She turned down all requests for help, but was adroit enough to do so in a manner that showed she was really thinking of the company's best interests. "Sure I could do that, Bill but I think Ralph should handle it. He really knows the area and this is a great opportunity for him to demonstrate leadership. Let's nurture him along." She always had a ready smile for everyone even though she had to really work at it, because she disliked most of her colleagues. She cut down rivals, but was careful to do so with innuendo and misdirection. Rather than overt attacks, she always made it a point to direct honeyed words to persons she had maligned discreetly. To matter how big corporations functioned and she dutifully toed the line. Now, it was time for her review. She expected to be made the division head. The company had recently instituted a new evaluation process, but she was not worried. Had she not gone out of her way to be "nice" to everyone, at all levels? The review was a shock—like walking unexpectedly into an ice cold shower. "Insensitive", "Does not listen or pay attention", "Self-absorbed", "Not a team player"—the feedback shocked her. "But . . . But . . . that's not true," she protested weakly as she tried to make the case that she was none of those things. "Yes, it is true, Sheila," John, the general manager responded kindly. "You go through the motions of compliance, but you are really out for yourself. You pretend to listen, but you are really trying to score points. People are not dummies. They sense this at a subliminal level. Everyone said something similar, so you really do have a problem. The good news is that they still like you because you do fine work. However, that will not last unless you change your attitude. Let's talk about what you need to do?" Did Sheila display the right attitude? Not at all. She was faking and people could clearly make out her put-on attitude.

When you approach a task with a positive attitude, you feel more alive, more enthusiastic and more committed. You improve your chances of success immeasurably. Your principal aim in life should be to cultivate positive attitudes, because you are unlikely to get far without them. To develop a positive attitude, there is a need to have a strategy. You need to think positive, stay focused and motivated. A two stage strategy should be adopted as given below:

- **Stage 1.** In this stage choose the attitude you want to change. It is advisable to make a journal and note down the reasons for wanting to change a particular attitude. Note down the benefits you will derive from its change. Positive self talk is essential for success. Moreover, positive affirmations help to keep your mind on track by not allowing any room for discouraging negative thoughts. Catherine Pulsifer rightly says, *"A positive attitude is definitely one of the keys to success. My definition of positive attitude is a simple one. Look for the good in all the circumstances."*

- **Stage 2.** Change requires a commitment of time. I will suggest that for 30 days don't watch negative shows or movies. Don't read negative articles in newspapers and magazines. Instead, read motivating articles or books, and associate with positive people.

To sum up, always have a positive outlook. Attitude is the sum total of your beliefs, assumptions, expectations and values. Attitude is defined as 'the way a person feels, thinks and behaves towards a particular issue'. Our thinking reflects from our actions/deads. When you approach a task with a positive attitude, you feel more alive, more enthusiastic and more committed. You improve your chances of success immeasurably. Your principal aim in life should be to cultivate positive attitude, because you're unlikely to get far without it.

"An optimist sees opportunity in every danger;
The pessimist sees danger in every opportunity."

—Winston Churchill

"When life hands you a lemon, make lemonade."

—Norman Vincent Peale

15

Manage Stress and Anger to Succeed

"The degree of one's emotions varies inversely
With one's knowledge of the facts."

—Bertrand Russell

Stress Management

Stress is a set of emotional and physical responses to the things happening in our life. It has physical and emotional effects on us and can create positive and negative feelings. As a positive influence, stress can compel us to take action. As a negative effect, stress can lead to health problems such as headaches, upset stomach, rashes, insomnia, ulcers, high blood pressure, heart diseases, stroke, etc. Stress is caused by self, others and the environment.

Have you experienced in you the following behaviour during the last few months? (Answer—Yes or No).

- Getting irritated easily.
- Loss of sleep and feeling tired.
- Losing your temper frequently.
- Feeling generally run down and hopeless.
- Altered eating pattern, loss of appetite or excessive eating.

- Frequent headache and indigestion.
- Difficulty in remembering things.
- Experience dramatic mood swings.
- Missing or being late for important appointments.
- Feeling burnt out.
- Frequently repeating in conversation.
- Panicking for small things.
- Frequently taking time off from work.
- Falling sick frequently.

If you have answered more than 3 *"yes"*, you need to take notice as it indicates that you are under stress.

You need to be aware of the causes of stress and triggers which always put you under stress. The reasons could be numerous or a few, depending upon your level of stress. Some of the reasons can be:

- Not having proper goals in life and not putting in enough effort towards the achievement of the goals.
- You may be overloaded with work and an additional to the misery could be that you are disorganized.
- There may be a tendency in you to procrastinate and not adhere to the deadlines set for achieving the tasks.
- Time planning may be faulty.
- Emotional instability and faulty decision making leads to pressure and uneasiness.
- Lack of life skills and unhealthy interpersonal relationships at home and at place of work.
- Having low self-esteem and lacking in confidence.
- People do not appreciate your worth.

- Environment in the office may be unhealthy. Environment factors like heavy traffic on the road, noise in and near your home add to the stress level.
- Lack of proper exercise and poor health.

Strategy to Cope with Stress

You should adopt a sound strategy to cope with stress. You could do the following:

- When you are under stress take deep breaths at least three times. Also stretch yourself or take a walk, laugh or smile.
- Ask yourself whether whatever is causing you to be stressed will matter to you, in any way in the near future.
- If you know you can't change things, tell yourself, "it's not worth worrying about, my well-being is more important". Always try to stay calm.
- Change your schedule to do something next which you have been looking forward to. Learn to prioritize your work and delegate whenever it is possible.
- Make sure you eat properly.
- Try relaxing or meditating techniques.
- Listen to some favourite music that is uplifting rather than depressing.
- Read an interesting book, watch a movie or your favourite TV programme.
- Think about happy times and memories. Always be positive and look to the future with hope.

Anger Management

Anger is an emotional state that varies in intensity from mild irritation to intense fury and rage. It is believed that moderate anger which results in positive outcome is good.

When you are angry, your heart beats faster and BP goes up. Anger can be caused by external and internal events, worrying and brooding over personal problems.

Poster of the Famous Movie Anger Management

Memories of traumatic events also cause anger. The goal of anger management is to reduce both your emotional feelings and physiological arousal that is caused by anger. You can't change things or people those enrage you, but you must learn to control your anger.

Why people get angry? People get angry easily when there is low tolerance for frustration, inconvenience or annoyance. This can also happen on being convicted for a minor mistake.

The following techniques will help in controlling anger:

- Carry out an analysis to find out what all triggers anger in you. Prepare a list and think of ways to overcome the causes of anger.

- When you are angry, try deep breathing and count to ten. You could also change your environment and repeat calm words like "relax", "calm down", etc. Learn to relax and calm your mind.
- If required, talk to people and tell them what makes you angry. You can seek their help.
- Physical exercise and meditation help to channelize aggressive tendencies.
- When you start getting angry, you could think of something positive or visualize something interesting you have experienced, e.g. enjoying summers on a hill station.
- You could let go off anger by speaking to the person who is the cause of your anger or writing a letter to let out your feelings. Of course, don't post the letter; tear it off.
- You should try to remain positive, patient and have control over your emotions. When angry, be careful of the words you use and also think about the worst consequences of anger. Learn to forgive and forget.

In the end, be aware of what causes stress and identify the triggers. When you are under stress, take deep breaths, switch over to pleasant thoughts, listen to soothing music or meditate. Exercise is a big stress buster. People who often get angry have low tolerance for frustration. They make unnecessary demands. Anger destroys peace and happiness in life. Learn to control your anger.

16

Believe in the Law of Attraction

"There is nothing that is against the law of attraction."
—Mathew Ward

Let me ask you a question, When do you feel good? WOW, that is very simple. Your answer will probably include: When I achieve something, get appreciated, people are kind to me and they value me, help others and get their help, give and receive something, I am in the company of good and positive people, etc, etc. Your list may contain many more reasons for you to feel good.

My next and final question, Why do you feel good in the above mentioned activities or situations? I am sure, I have set you to think. It's a secret no more; the Law of Attraction is working for you.

Many a time, you may have realized certain events taking place as soon as you think about them. At times, you may have thought of a friend and presto and he arrives at your house or you receive a call from him. Remember, it's the law of attraction which is working for you. What is this Law of Attraction?

The Law of Attraction states, "Like attracts like". It is a universal law which ensures that whatever energy is broadcasted out into the universe is attracted to energies that are of an equal and harmonious frequency, resonance or vibration. Thereafter, this multiplied energy returns to its source.

A brief explanation of this law is required. According to the Law, the thoughts we think emit frequencies. When you think, thoughts are sent into the universe and they attract like things that are on the same frequency. Thereafter, this multiplied energy comes back to its source. So, when you think good or positive it makes you feel better as the law of attraction is continuously working.

This universal law is working in your life right now, whether you are aware of it or not. You are attracting the situations, the people, the career you want and many more into your life. Once you are aware of this law and how it works, you can use it, to manifest what you want in your life. **To create what you want, you need to follow three steps, which are: Ask, Believe, and** Receive.

- Ask the Universe what you want. Be very clear on what you really want.
- Believe you have already received, what you have asked for. This involves acting, speaking, and thinking that the want has been fulfilled.
- Receive involves, feeling the way you will feel once your desire has manifested.

When you emit the frequencies of having received and feel that the desire has been fulfilled, the law of attraction takes over. It moves people, events, and circumstances for you to receive. Also, you get inspired to plan and take right actions. Mike Doodley has this to say about the law, " If you can think about what is in your mind, and make that your dominant thought, you will bring it into your life. This way thoughts become things." My Grandpa used to say, *"What you think, it happens."*

The Law of Attraction is a very powerful law. To realize your dreams, it is important for you to have positive thoughts and feelings. Further, when you believe in abundance and practice gratitude, you are actually sending out powerful energy into the universe. Well, now you know the secret—Law of Attraction.

Believe in Abundance

The Law of Abundance can be best understood by looking at the continual growth and unlimited resources available within our universe. It is continuously producing and multiplying effortlessly through the power of the above universal law. There are simple things we can do to live in abundance. Here are some of them:

Let abundance flow in your life

There is enough for you to have everything you need. Resentment, jealousy, envy and self-pity interfere with the freeflow of abundance.

Don't fill up your life with things you really don't want

Ask yourself if you want the thing before you buy it.

Be grateful and focus on the good that is already in your life

It's easy to think about what you don't have but thinking

about what you do have, will really make you feel good.

You must realize the power of giving and receiving

Every time you freely give money away or help someone in any form, you are implying that you are confident that more will come to you. This is a big positive affirmation with a lot of power behind it. Similarly, being able to receive from other people is healthy; it gives other people the pleasure of giving.

Forgiving those who have wronged you is part of living abundantly

Holding onto your anger, resentments, insults, etc. however justifiable they may seem, keeps you stuck in the past, rather than letting you move forward into a better future.

You may ask, "Why isn't everybody living the life of their dreams?" The reason why people don't have what they want is because they are thinking more about what they don't want than what they want. The law of attraction doesn't compute, "don't, or not or no", or any other word of negation. Example: If you speak, "I don't want to fall sick", this is what the law of attraction is receiving, "I want to fall sick."

Gratitude Will Change Your Life

Have you ever found yourself in a state when you just don't feel good about anything? Try to be grateful and that will dramatically change not only your outlook but also your reality.

There are reasons why gratitude is so powerful. When you put yourself into the energy of gratitude, you are flowing some of the **highest vibrative energy possible.**

So what happens when you start to flow that positive energy? **It goes out and returns multiplied by the law of attraction.** Gratitude can make you focus on good things of life, change your perspective and lead you towards what you really want.

When you continue to find something to be grateful for, you'll keep on feeling better. **The more you express thanks, more of the same, you will get back.**

Gratitude raises your awareness. You begin to notice all the things that are there in your life to be appreciated. And the more you appreciate, the more you become aware of them.

There are many methods to express gratitude. This can be done by making a gratitude list, expressing thanks, visualizing good things and feeling good.

I'm sure you have now realized that it is important to have positive thoughts and expectations of what you want, and not of what you don't want. Always, think good about yourself and for others too. Let the law of attraction work for you. Believe in abundance and be grateful for what you have. In case you want to know more about the law of attraction, I recommend you to read the beautiful book, "The Secret" by Rhonda Byrne.

THE BEST LAW OF ATTRACTION QUOTES

- ☐ "Have an attitude of gratitude in all that you do."
- ☐ "Energy flows where attention goes."
- ☐ "Do not give others the chance to create your happiness."
- ☐ "Gratitude is awareness."
- ☐ "Success is something you attract."
- ☐ "Stand tall in your own eyes."
- ☐ "Don't major in minor things."
- ☐ "Believe in abundance and be happy."
- ☐ "Language, it says a lot about you."
- ☐ "To have more, you have to become more."
- ☐ "Happiness is not the cause of gratitude..."

  "It is the result!"

17

Improve your Communication Skills to Achieve Success

"You can have brilliant ideas, but if you can't get them across, Your ideas won't get you anywhere."

—*Lee Iacocca*

Who is your favourite actor? What do you like about him? In your answer you will name him and add that he has a great personality which means that his appearance is good, he has a charming voice and can express himself well. Also, he is law abiding, obedient and is also a great communicator.

Good communication skills are vital for achieving success. The ability to convey information, instructions, views and feelings in a clear and concise manner is important to achieve the desired results. Technology has contributed tremendously towards faster and efficient communication. You can acquire great knowledge but unless you communicate to others, it is worthless. A good communicator does his job well, works in harmony

with others, feels motivated and earns respect and trust of all.

We communicate with others either orally [verbal and non-verbal], in written form or through media [video, tv, posters etc.]

Quiz: Communication skills: To know your proficiency in communication skills in the statements given below, mark your response; Always, Often, Sometimes, Rarely, Never.

- I give full attention when people are talking to me.
- I encourage people to talk.
- I present my ideas so that others are receptive to my point of view.
- I treat people and family with respect.
- I value teamwork.
- I show respect to other's ideas.
- I try to understand people.
- I am open to feedback.
- I win people's trust and respect.
- I check and make sure, I have understood what other people are trying to communicate.
- I am confident at giving a presentation.
- I avoid making absolute judgments.
- I honour my commitments.

Score. Give points, **Always–5, Often–4, Sometimes–3, Rarely–2 and Never–1.**

Add. If you score:

50 and over :	You are an exceptional communicator.
Between 40 to 49:	You tend to be a very good communicator.
Between 36 to 39:	You will benefit from polishing your skills.
Under 30 :	You possess underdeveloped skills, take action to improve your communication skills.

Listening Skills

To be a good communicator, you must learn the art of listening. Listening involves hearing, seeing and feeling. Epictetus said, *"We have two ears and one mouth so that we can listen twice as much as we speak."* Good listeners are patient, flexible and openminded. Here are a few tips to improve your listening skills.

- Maintain eye contact with the person who is communicating with you.
- Remember not to interrupt until the other person pauses, or invites you to speak.
- Be interested in what's being said. Even if it doesn't sound interesting, it might turn out to be better later on. Also, be open-minded and concentrate on what is being said.
- Remember every person has the right to express his/her thoughts/opinions even if you disagree. Resist temptation to anticipate.
- Help the speaker by nodding, smiling etc. Pay attention to his/her body language.

Body Language at Work

Body language refers to non-verbal signals we send and receive, intentionally or unintentionally. Every aspect of our face to face communication is influenced by body language, which can back what we say or reinforce it or it can contradict our words. We must ensure that our body language matches with the words we speak.

The words we utter and the tone we use account for 35 per cent of our communication while the body language staggers 65 per cent. There lies the power and effectiveness of body language. The elements of body language can be categorized as under:

Personal Appearance

It includes physique, attractiveness, personal hygiene, hair-style and even skin tone.

Posture

It is the way we stand, sit and walk. An individual's state of mind can be made out by the position of his hands and legs.

Eye Contact

The eyes are considered as a window to an individual's mind. Eyes are used maximum while we are communicating with people. We can be assessed based upon how we use our eyes.

Gestures

Well timed gestures enhance impact. Threatening gestures must be avoided at all times.

Facial Expressions

It is believed that 15,000 signals are conveyed by the face alone. To look cheerful, confident and an attractive person, you must learn to smile. Don't blink eyes, bite lips, tighten jaw muscles, touch nose or hair. Remember, even thoughts can influence facial expressions.

Space Distance

It indicates the type of relationship. The distance will be less when relationship is a close one, and it will be more informal relationship.

Voice

The tone, volume, pitch, pace and pause have tremendous bearing on communication. Remember, what we say and how you say has a great impact.

Open and Closed Body Language

A characteristic of an effective body language is its openness. By keeping your gestures away from your body you indicate that you have nothing to hide, and you show acceptance of others and a willingness to interact with them.

Barrier Positions

If you fold your body, you will be assumed as being defensive. Your arms form a protective guard in front of you, as if you are responding to an attack. This is the position we sometimes assume when we disagree with what is being said, and are not going to budge from our point of view.

Signals of Power

There are certain postures and mannerisms that are seen to indicate a superior or patronizing attitude. You must be aware of the meanings of various body postures.

- **Ways of Sitting.** Sitting with the leg over one arm of the chair may, in some contexts, be a casual relaxed position. But mostly in working situations such a position communicates extreme self-confidence or superiority over the other person.
- **Ways of Standing.** Towering over someone can appear threatening as its an exaggeratedly upright stance. A pose that indicates superior status is standing tall with the hands clasped behind the back and the head held high. Other posture that can indicate superiority is standing with hands on waist with the elbows jutting out.

Gestures and Mannerisms

Folded arms can give a confrontational impression, as can habits such as pointing a finger. Fist closing can show sign of hostility and can be an aggressive action.

Developing the kind of body language that displays confidence in yourself and others will help you to manage working situations effectively. Open body gestures, posture that is upright but relaxed, steady eye contact and clear hand gestures are examples of assertive non-verbal signals.

How to Recognize Aggressive and Assertive Body Language?

Body Language	*Aggressive*	*Assertive*
• Eye contact	Staring	Good contact without staring
• Facial expression	Chin forward, gritting of teeth/ jaw, frowning, narrowing of the eyes	Open interested expression, smiling genuinely
• Movements and gestures	Bold, forceful movements, finger pointing, head/ face pushed forward, thumping fist, tapping fingers	Open gestures, head tilted when listening, and positive hand movements
• Positioning	Invading your space, leaning forward, posed aggressively	Appropriate distance between people, leaning towards other person
• Voice	Loud, rising at the end of the sentence, sarcastic, very firm	Clear, firm, steady, sincere

You must have understood the importance of good communication skills. You must learn the art of listening. Be open-minded and concentrate on what is being said. While communicating with people, you must ensure that your body language matches with spoken words.

Awareness of open and closed body gestures will help

you to understand people better and you will be able to convey your viewpoint effectively. Use assertive body language but avoid aggressiveness.

> *The most imortant thing in communication is*
> *Hearing what isn't being said.*
>
> ***—Tenzing Gyatso***
>
> *I like to listen.*
> *I have learned a great deal*
> *From listening carefully.*
> *Most people never listen.*
>
> ***—Andre Gire***
>
> *Listen to many,*
> *Speak to a few.*
>
> ***—William Shakespeare***

18

The Basic Laws Governing Relationships

"Personal relationships are the fertile soil from which all Advancements, achievements, and success in real life grow."

—Ben Stein

People are happiest when they have wonderful relationships with the people they love. The secret principle of human nature is the craving for appreciation. People are needed for support, encouragement, for ideas and friendship. Your ability to get along with people is an indication of who you are and how you feel about yourself. It is important that people must feel comfortable in your company. Your respect for yourself enables you to do right things and you are bound to have good relationships, which will lead to a happy life. In a relationship caring is achieved by having faith, openness and empathy with others. Also, do not expect the other person to change just because you want him to change.

There are some basic laws which govern relationships, with your partner or spouse, your children, friends, neighbours, working colleagues and even a complete stranger. Understanding and mastering the basic laws will help you to get on well with everyone.

Mutual Fulfillment of Needs

If you fulfill the their own needs, the other person will want to maintain and deepen their relationship with you. These needs can be physical, practical or emotional. Attention, loyalty, fun, affection, companionship, moral support, appreciation and so on, are basic to human survival. Think about it, will you want to spend time with someone who always talks without giving you a chance to speak? You must learn to satisfy your needs. The satisfaction of your emotional needs should be given priority. Keep in mind that there are hundreds of different needs. Need to control others, dominate, or manage, to share, be heared, to be free and selfreliant are some of the important needs. You should pick two or three needs at a time and find out ways to satisfy them.

Express your Expectations

People enter into relationships primarily because they want to feel good. They want to feel noticed, valued and safe. In addition, most of them expect to be heard, recognized, approved and appreciated. Don't assume that people should know what your expectations are. Take responsibility to express your expectations. However, your expectations should be easily achievable, otherwise, you may have to face disappointment.

Take Responsibility for putting the Relationship Right

If you want a relationship to succeed, approach it with the attitude of putting something in it rather than getting something out of it. Make people feel special and important. Don't blame others if a relationship is not going well; take responsibility for putting it right.

Have Genuine Interest

Are you genuinely interested in other people? By taking a genuine interest in other people, all your relationships can become enormously gratifying. Your inner feelings are visible in many subtle ways by posture, facial expression, voice tone, gesture, etc. If you're pretending to be interested in others, thy may know that. The most popular people genuinely like and care for others. They give off positive 'vibes'. Develop a bona-fide, open, caring and friendly attitude.

Good Communication Skills

The basis of all relationships is good communication skills. People react differently. They rarely will view the world in the same way as others do. Remember, it's not the event but your way of responding that determines your response to an outcome.

Relate to others on Emotional Level

A major step in getting on well with people is to understand and respect their feelings, no matter how unreasonable and groundless they may seem. Human beings are emotional creatures. We are more inclined to respond emotionally than logically. Sometimes our emotional impulses work to our advantage, but they can also spell disaster if we dismiss another person's point of view. People want to feel good. Knowing how to make others feel good emotionally, is the key to good relationships.

Give Encouragement and Positive Feedback

You must encourage others so that they can improve themselves and become confident and lead a balanced life. Make a compliment or a positive feedback the focal point of your communication rather than a passing comment.

Ask for Help

You should always know what you want. Somehow we have this crazy notion that it is not good to seek help. You will be surprized to know that many people are ready to help you; only because they do not know as to what you require. Only when you interact with them and ask for help, you will get help from them.

Forgive and Forget the Past Unpleasantness

Nearly every day in our lives, we run into people who are unpleasant, obnoxious and downright nasty. It could be on the road, in the supermarket, in the workplace or any other location where we come into contact with people with differing views. If we hold on to the nasty comments of other people or our own, over time they will swell into a river of negative thoughts. Therefore, it is best to forgive and forget the past unpleasantness.

Networking with People

Build a strong network of special friends who can support you. Be in the company of successful people. You could also think of creating your own mastermind group. In this group, members should support each other and work for overall success. The best way to start attracting great people towards you is to stop being judgmental about others and yourself. Bearing a grudge or being angry is a large energy drain.

A farmer, Mr. Fleming, saved a boy's life. Next day a well dressed gentleman arrived at the farmer's hut. The gentleman wanted to reward the farmer as he had saved his son's life. The farmer said that he had done his duty and don't want any reward. The gentleman noticed a boy in rags. He asked the farmer about the boy. He happened to be the farmer's son. He requested the farmer to let him take responsibility of the child's education. The boy grew up to become a famous scientist. His name was Alexander Fleming who invented penicillin. Few years later the gentleman's son suffered a severe attack of pneumonia. His life was saved by the penicillin injection. Isn't it great! The farmer and the gentleman developed perfect human relationship based upon mutual respect and dignity for each other.

You should do good without expecting anything in return. You will reap the benefit in some way or the other. The very act of doing good is a reward by itself.

Where do all our relationships exist? Well the answer is not difficult, **"relationships exist in our thoughts."** They are what you imagine. You always view your relationships through the lens of your experience and perception. Love others as you love yourself and treat them the way you like to be treated. Be courteous, friendly and always have a smile on your face. Always be truthful without any offence. Hold the other person and yourself to high and noble standards.

To sum up, relationships play an important role in achievement of success. Basic laws of relationships must be put into practice. Try to understand and fulfil the needs of other people and yours too. Have genuine interest and take responsibility to build-up solid relationships.

19

You are very Lucky if you have True Friends

"A true friend is one who overlooks your failures
And tolerates your successes."

—Doug Larson

You must nurture friendship with like minded people who know how to enjoy life. Let your friends know that you are willing to be there when they need you. Visit someone you haven't seen for a long time. We succeed with the help of others. People grow by growing together. If you'd like to have many friends, then share friendship with others generously. Abraham Lincoln said, "The better part of one's life consists of his friendships".

Friends nurture us when we are in pain, console us when we grieve and share our delight when we rejoice. Ralph Waldow Emerson's view on friendship is, "To have a good friend, you must be one." Here is a story which brings out the virtues of friends.

Two friends were walking through a desert. At some point of the journey they had an argument, and one friend slapped the other on the face. The one who was slapped was hurt, but without saying anything, he wrote on the sand: **Today my best friend slapped me on the face**. They kept on walking until they reached an oasis, where they decided to take a bath. The one who had been slapped got stuck in the mire and started drowning, but his friend saved him. After he recovered, he wrote on a stone: **Today my best friend saved my life**. The friend who had slapped and saved his best friend asked him, "After I hurt you, you wrote in the sand and now you write on a stone, why?" The other friend replied, "When someone hurts us we should write it down on sand where winds of forgiveness can erase it away. But, when someone does something good for us, we must engrave it in stone where no wind can ever erase it."

To blossom, friendship requires many qualities such as unselfishness, genuine care for other person, etc. When you show respect and gratitude to your friends, you will be blessed in untold ways. You should work gradually in friendship and build rapport gradually. To have good friends you must keep the following in mind:

- You should love your friends and never criticize them unjustly. Look for goodness and encourage them to improve their life. Ralph Waldo Emerson has very aptly said, **"He who has a thousand friends has not a friend to spare, while who has one enemy shall meet him everywhere."**
- Have friendship with people who are optimistic in life. Remember, having a good personality will help you to win friends and influence people.
- Be fully committed in your friendship.
- Take personal responsibility. It requires you to accept your mistake.
- Be honest in your dealings and always look at things with a positive mind.

- Build trust and mutual respect.
- You need to resist the temptation of always pleasing people. Don't overload yourself by taking on tasks of others. Recognize when it is appropriate to say "NO."

Keep Away from Foolish Friends

I am tempted to narrate one of my favourite stories from the bedtime stories my father used to tell. Once upon a time, a clever monkey lived in a tree that bore juicy, red rose apples. He was very happy. One fine day, a crocodile swam up to that tree and told the monkey that he had travelled a long distance and was in search of food. The kind monkey offered him a few rose apples. The crocodile enjoyed them very much and asked the monkey whether he could come again for some more fruit. The generous monkey happily agreed. The crocodile returned the next day. Soon the two became very good friends. They discussed their lives, their friends and family, like all friends do. The crocodile told the monkey that he had a wife and that they lived on the other side of the river. So the kind monkey offered him some extra apples to take home for his wife. The crocodile's wife loved the apples and made her husband promise to get her a few every day.

Meanwhile, the friendship between the monkey and the crocodile deepened as they spent more and more time together. The crocodile's wife started feeling jealous. She wanted to put an end to this friendship. So she pretended that she could not believe that her husband could be friend to a monkey. Her husband tried to convince her that he and the monkey shared a true friendship.

The crocodile's wife then thought to herself that if the monkey lived on a diet of rose apples, his flesh would be very sweet. So she thought of a plan. One day, she pretended to be very ill and told the crocodile that the doctor said that she would only recover if she ate a monkey's heart. If her husband wanted to save her life, he must bring her his friend's heart. The crocodile was aghast. He was in a dilemma. On the one hand, he loved his friend. On the other, he could not possibly let his wife die. The crocodile's wife threatened him saying that if he did not get her the monkey's heart, she would surely die.

The crocodile went to the rose apple tree and invited the monkey to his home to meet his wife. He told the monkey that he could ride across the river on his back. The monkey happily agreed. As they reached the middle of the river, the crocodile began to sink. The frightened monkey asked him why he was doing that. The crocodile explained that he would have to kill the monkey to save his wife's life. The clever monkey told him that he would gladly give his heart to save the life of the crocodile's wife, but he had left his heart behind on the rose apple tree. He asked the crocodile to make haste and turn back so that he could go and get his heart from the apple tree. The silly crocodile quickly swam back to the rose apple tree. The monkey scampered up the tree to safety. He told the crocodile that he was a foolish friend.

Friendship is a gift of enormous value. It provides intimacy, rapport, trust and affection. Trust is built by honouring your commitments, helping friends when they are in need and accepting them as they are. It is important to choose friends wisely and keep away from those who are not trust-worthy and foolish. French poet Jacques Delille wrote, "Our relatives are ours by chance, but we choose our friends." How true it is! you have a wide choice. However, don't use it too often.

In a nutshell, you must have friends who respect and value you. Have a good network of friends and don't hesitate to ask for help when required. People are ready to help, state clearly as to what you want. To have a good friend you must yourself be one.

You know, to have a good friend, you yourself need to be. Here is a joke about a spinster. She was asked by her friend as to why she did not get married.

Spinster replied, "You see, I was looking for a perfect husband."

Friend asked, "Did you find one?"

Spinster nodded her head and said, "Yes!

Dear, I did find one."

"Then why didn't you marry him?" asked the puzzled friend.

After taking a deep breath and looking towards the open sky, the spinster softly said, "Oh, he was looking for a perfect wife!"

20

What does Success Mean to you?

"Success does not consist in never making blunders,
But never making the same one a second time."

—Josh Billings

Every human being looks forward to lead a successful and happy life. Success is achieved by a systematic and deliberate process of deciding what to do with life. What you will do when you get there and what steps are necessary to get you where you want to be. Remember, achieving success without happiness is meaningless. Happiness is achieved by looking forward to, by sharing and by making somebody else happy. It is observed that success means different things to different people.

- To some it may be accumulation of wealth.
- To someone else it may be attaining a high position like becoming a minister in the government or head of a prestigious organisation.

- To someone it may be having a great family and living in harmony with others.
- To some it may be as simple as earning enough which gives them adequate food and security.

What does Success Mean to you?

The meaning of success comes in many forms and has many definitions based on individual perspectives. Here are some of them.

- Success depends on what you are searching in your life. Athletes may have one definition of success whereas a musician may look at success by producing a hit album. True success is to be passion driven and achieved by positive actions.
- Success is the completion of anything intended or planned for; it could be about developing oneself into a person who is valuable to others. It is an accomplishment of an aim or purpose in one's life.
- To be successful means to be truly peaceful and know how to return to a state of peace when disturbed.
- Success is the ability to go from one failure to another without loss of enthusiasm. Never give up because you may be only one step away from success.
- If you call yourself happy, you can call yourself successful.
- The art of success is based on a clear understanding and implementation of the natural process of thought. It is the manifestation of effective thought, focused by passion.
- Success is learned skills. It's not just something that we are born with naturally. It is the identification and moulding of our natural talents and abilities.

- Success has to be both inward and outward. What the outside world can see and measure could be an achievement on the career ladder, material wealth, or reaching top spot in sports, science or any field. Whereas, inward success is achievement of integrity, moral values, confidence, self-esteem and respect for others.

Success Story of Bill Gates

Bill Gates when asked about his secret of success by a TV reporter, replied that he followed a five point formula:

- Passion generates focus which is essential for success. When you recognize your real hidden talent and work to develop that, you become passionate and get self-motivated to work hard.
- Make yourself intelligent. This basically will involve acquiring knowledge from books, internet and other sources.
- Whatever you do must be done with sincere effort. Remember, integrity is important, whether in business or family life.
- Create talented teams if you want to rise in business. Lead your people to victory by providing good leadership and motivate them to achieve the targets.
- Have proper reward and punishment to keep the work force united. Once you start understanding and knowing various benchmarks of success, you start moving towards success in life.

Successful people have a dream and a plan to achieve it. Study of successful people reveals that they have appropriate skills, talents, and characteristics that enable them to succeed.

Characteristics you'll find in successful people are:

- Successful people have a dream, ambition and are strongly motivated towards its achievement.
- Successful people are focused, they know how to get things done and take responsibility to support their actions.
- Successful people look for solutions to the problem, make sound decisions and have the courage to admit their mistakes.
- Successful people are self-reliant. They have specific knowledge, training, and/or skills and talents related to what they want to achieve.
- Successful people are enthusiastic. They understand people they work with and co-operate with them.

In a nutshell, the meaning of success comes in various forms. It could be to achieve something, lead a smooth and peaceful life, being happy and so on. To succeed in life you need to have the right mental attitude, acquire new skills, be ready to learn from your failures and make success a habit.

21

Good Health leads to Happiness

"It is health that is real wealth, and not pieces of gold and silver."

—Mahatma Gandhi

Healthy people have lot of energy and they outperform those who are unhealthy. The importance of health is realized only when you fall sick or when you enter old age. There is a famous saying, **"A healthy body carries a healthy mind."** Take care of your health. It should be your top priority. Your body is powered by the energy it receives, from the food you eat, exercizing the body, water you drink, laughter, etc. To remain healthy and happy, you should remember the following:

Exercise your Body

To combat disease and aging, you need to keep your bones, joints and muscles flexible and strong. The right exercise includes weight-bearing exercise and not simply aerobics. It will do you good if you take a brisk walk for thirty to forty minutes daily. In addition, yoga and meditation will not only give you exercise but also help you to have a cool and peaceful mind.

Have Adequate Sleep

To keep yourself healthy, you must have daily 6 to 8 hours of sleep. Take rest to rejuvenate when you are tired. Have a break from your busy schedule and remember the good old saying, **"Sometimes you must stop to smell a rose."** I am reminded of what I was told by my elders, **"Early to bed, early to rise, makes a man healthy, wealthy and wise."**

Eating Habits

Proper nutrition is very important. You must eat the right kind of food and stay away from fast food or junk food. You are doing yourself and your children a dangerous, long-term disservice by developing the habit of eating high fat nutritioned poor meals. What you eat has a major impact on degenerative diseases. To remain healthy, ensure the following:

- **Eat a low fat and low sugar diet**. Keep your fat intake to 15 per cent of all daily calories. This will keep you lean and boost your immunity. Always eat a low-sugar diet. Use a little fructose in place of table sugar.
- **Eat a low salt diet.** Use a potassium-based salt as substitute.
- **Eat a high-fibre diet.** Fibre protects the colon from cancer, lowers cholesterol and stabilizes blood sugar. Eat 40 to 50 grams of mixed fibres daily. Whole grain breads and cereals, especially those containing oat bran, vegetables and fruits have a high fibre context.
- **Supplement diet with nutrients.** You should take daily nutritional supplements including essential vitamins, antioxidants and minerals. Current research confirms that we can no longer get the essential nutrients from our food alone. We must supplement even the best diet with nutrients to promote resistance to diseases.

- **Drink clean water**. Drink bottled or home distilled water, minimum eight glasses per day. The benefits of water are tremendous. Drinking water quenches thirst, aids digestion, cools your body during exercise, flushes out waste and carries essential nutrients to your body's cells. Water also reduces the risks of kidney stones, lubricates joints, improves skin tone, relieves headaches, and curbs appetite and snacking.

Laughter Therapy

Laughing makes you feel happy, healthy and brainy. We change physiologically when we laugh. We stretch muscles throughout our face and body, and we breathe faster, sending more oxygen to our tissues. In the last few decades, researchers have studied laughter's effects on the body and churned out some interesting information on how not only it affects us positively but also the people around us.

- **Blood Flow.** Researchers at the University of Maryland studied the effects on blood vessels when people were shown either comedies or dramas. After screening, the blood vessels of the group who had watched the comedy behaved normally. Their flow were expanding and contracting easily. But the blood vessels in people who had watched the drama tended to tense up, restricting the blood flow.
- **Blood Sugar Levels.** The study of 19 people with diabetes looked at the effects of laughter on blood sugar levels. After eating, the group attended a tedious lecture. On the next day, the group ate the same meal and then watched a comedy. After the comedy, the group had lower blood sugar levels than they had after the lecture.

The Power of Smile

It is something you can give to a friend and to a stranger too. It seems that when you give it, it's given back to you. This gift is worth a million but doesn't cost a paisa. It's lasting in effect but doesn't take much time. This simple little gesture can make the day worthwhile. My daughter has a huge hanging in her room which says, **"Smile a lot. It costs nothing."** How true!

In a nutshell, good health leads to happiness. Your body is provided energy by the food you eat, exercises you do, water you drink and positive aspects of laughter therapy. Ralph Waldo Emerson has described good health as, "Health is a state of complete mental and social well-being, and not merely absence of diseases or infirmity."

> *"Age is an issue of mind over matter.*
> *If you don't mind... It doesn't matter."*
>
> ***—Mark Twain***

22

To Live a Super Life, Be Happy

"If a man speaks or acts with pure thoughts,
Happiness follows him like a shadow."

—Buddha

My uncle used to say, **"Success and happiness are kid brothers"**. He was of the opinion that success which does not lead to happiness, is of no use. He would narrate stories of rich people who were unhappy due to various reasons. A successful person may not be really happy, but a happy person will invariably achieve success.

We can not be happy solely on the basis of external factors but it has to come from within. There are people who have everything they desire, yet are unhappy. To be happy, choose your emotions and thoughts. Free yourself from past baggage, mistakes and regrets. Learn to live life to the full and look hopefully at the future. We should learn to appreciate good times as well as bad times. Robin Sharma says, **"Don't label situations as good or bad. When**

unhappiness confronts you, rather than running away, exercise the force of will to run through it. It's not just in thought but in actions too".

If you think that your happiness is in someone else's hands, you are in for trouble. Since true happiness is from within, try to achieve inner peace. The inner self is based on patterns and habits. Therefore, try to break the patterns and change the habits. To remain happy, try to keep your mind away from worries and avoid mental clutter.

No Worry

How to Live a Happy Life?

To be happy in life, you should try to live life as the "real you". Happiness is an emotion, a feeling. You can achieve happiness from one simple intention and also by making others happy.

Happy People

To be happy in life, keep encouraging yourself and tackle the "inner critic", the voice inside your head which encourages or demoralizes you. Every time you hear the critic, interrupt it with words of encouragement.

Happiness is a feeling which is enjoyed while you are in the present moment. Do not waste your time in the past, especially in your mistakes or unhappy moments. Think positive, enjoy and have fun in the present.

Everyone wants to be happy, yet many people think that their happiness is based solely on wealth. Thousands of years ago, King Solomon accumulated wealth more than anyone in history and experienced more pleasures than most people can imagine. Despite his wealth and power, King Solomon felt empty. Wealth does make life easy and yet it's not end of all.

Always be optimistic and tell yourself, "Today is a great day", and then do what's necessary to make your expectations come true. Do those things which will make you feel happy, e.g., playing the guitar, listening to music, watching nature, etc. Play to your strengths and do things that make you feel wonderful. Find time to enjoy what you like and appreciate. Always keep smiling and project a happy appearance.

Do things to show that you love your family and friends as they matter to you. It could be one phone call, sending greetings on a happy occasion and so on. Try to shed the burden of judgment and you will feel much better. When you judge, you cut off understanding and shut down the process of love. Always try to look for positives in people.

Spend quality time with your family and friends. Further, keep looking for opportunities to help others. This will give lots of satisfaction and will make you feel happy.

Do you know that we can express the secret of happiness in mathematical terms?

H = R/N, where H stands for happiness, R for resources and N for your needs.

As the quantum of your needs starts decreasing the 'H' quotient keeps increasing. If you can bring down the 'N' factor to zero, 'H' reaches infinity. Such a feat is almost impossible for the average people. Most of the people live their lives assuming that existing resources are insufficient to fulfil their needs. This economic thought process leads to 'scarcity' and so there arises conflict.

A friend of mine used to define happiness by the following mathematic formula:

$$\textbf{Happiness} = \frac{\text{Number of desires fulfilled}}{\text{Number of desires entertained}}$$

Happiness Tools in Pursuit of Happiness

We must have gone wrong somewhere for happiness seems to have become a rare commodity. Do we really know what makes us happy? A successful person by society's standards is not necessarily a happy person. Genuine happiness is a statement of contentment that comes with peace of mind and a sense of well-being. It is regardless of outward circumstances. Given below are certain tools which will make you feel happy.

Personal Power

This is the almost definable proactive force that gives you power over your feelings and your fate. Personal power has two components: taking responsibility and taking action. It means realizing that your life belongs to you and you alone, and then doing something about it. Personal power keeps you from being a victim. When your personal power is at its peak, you can handle whatever life dishes out.

Choices

During your life your time, have to make number of choices. You have the freedom to choose your response to any situation or an event. You can be furious and edgy with the demands and pressures of a hectic day, find faults with weather and whatever. Well, you can also respond by being cool and focusing your mind on positive aspects of life.

Encouragement and Appreciation

This is the most important tool of happiness. Encouragement and appreciation is the purest and strongest form of love. It is the outward bound kind of love that asks for nothing and gives everything. When you find time to go for a walk, dance, sing your favourite tune or share happy moments with special people, "happy hormones" flood your system. This, in turn, makes you feel good about yourself and become happy.

Focus on your Strengths

When you take the path of the intellect and spirit, you naturally begin to focus on your strengths. Leading by your strengths makes you feel good, and that's why it works. Simple but true. You'll never be complete until you learn to lead with your strengths everyday.

Lead a Balanced Life

There are three primary components of life, namely relationships, health and work. You must try to put your energy in these components to live a balanced life.

> Here is an interesting story on happiness. Long ago in a small, far away village, there was a place known as the House of 1000 Mirrors. A small, happy little boy learned of this place and decided to visit. As he arrived, he walked happily up the stairs to the doorway of the house. He looked through the doorway. To his great surprise, he found himself staring at 1000 other happy little boys. He smiled a great smile, and was answered with 1000 great smiles, just as warm and friendly. As he left the House, he thought to himself, "This is a wonderful place. I will come back and visit it often."

In this same village, another little boy, who was not quite as happy as the first one, decided to visit the house. He slowly climbed the stairs and hung his head low as he looked into the door. When he saw the 1000 unfriendly looking faces staring back at him, he shouted at them and was horrified to see 1000 little boys shouting back at him. As he left, he thought to himself, "That is a horrible place, and I will never go back there again."

All the faces in the world are mirrors. What kind of reflections do you see in the faces of the people you meet? It all depends upon you, as your happiness is a reflection in the faces of the other person. The secret is, to remain happy in all types of situations.

In a nutshell, happiness is a state of mind. You should always remain happy by focusing your thoughts in the present and having a positive belief system. To be happy, live life as a "real you". You must encourage yourself and take care of the "inner critic." Happiness is not solely based on wealth. There are so many other factors which contribute to it. Remember the mathematical equation H=R/N. To increase your level of happiness, decrease the number of your needs. You have the personal power and choices to turn you into a happy person. Always focus on your strengths and lead a balanced life. If you do that, you are a genius.

When you achieve both success and happiness, you are genius person. Success and happiness are two things that all people aspire for. Both are mutually interwined. So, one can say that success brings happiness and happiness is an essential ingredient towards success. Thomas A Edison said, **"Men give me credit for being some genius. All the genius**

I have is this, when I have a subject in mind, I study it profoundly. Day and night it is before me. My mind becomes pervaded with it. The success I achieve, is what people are pleased to call the fruit of a genius. But I say, it is the fruit of labour and thought."

23

Help your Child to Succeed in School

"The future belongs to those who believe in the beauty of their dreams."

—Eleanor Roosevelt

We have been taught since ages that genes have a profound effect on, who we are, and what we do. If someone excels in a particular field, we attribute his achievements based on his genes. We often hear, "He must be gifted," "Good genes", "Innate ability" and "natural born." In the recent years, this myth has been busted. Studies have revealed that we develop traits through the dynamic process of gene and environment interaction (G × E). Yes, genes do play a role but it is the environment which plays greater role in shaping of geniuses. Here is a true story which highlights that you can train your child to be a genius. It is only a matter of the right strategies and methods.

Napoleon Bonaparte was mocked by his companions for his humble origins and poverty. He responded by studying harder, and soon became the best student in the class. Later, he went on to become one of the greatest generals in history.

Student's aim in School should be to gain knowledge and

do well in studies. Also, take steps to develop all round personality. He should take active part in extra curricular activities and/or excel in some sport. He should be popular and have a large number of good friends. You may have noticed that in school when a student consistently does exceptionally well in his studies, he is respected and at times hailed as a genius. Let's look at what a genius at school does:

- A genius person has intelligence, enthusiasm and endurance to acquire good results. Many people are of the view that genius also means being a great person.
- Intelligence means, the student has a good memory. It is not inborn but can be developed over a period of time. This is achieved by total focus, attention and understanding of the subjects. Intelligence can be improved through effort. It is with practice, training and above all applying various learning methods; we become more intelligent than we were before.
- Enthusiasm is a trait which is the outcome of perceived or actual attainment of success. When you do well in a subject, it automatically arouses your interest and you pay more attention to it. This enthusiasm can diminish when you don't get good results. I would advise you not lose heart but take it up as a challenge. Spend more time on your weaknesses, understand, analyse and seek help from others. Never let your enthusiasm die as it has a direct affect on your way of thinking and taking action. You need to know yourself, in terms of your strengths and weaknesses. Work on them and have a high level self esteem and confidence.

- Endurance means being persistent, never giving up and be able to surmount difficulties in your school life. It also means taking stalk of your time and avoiding procrastination. You would have to sacrifice some ordinary pleasures like watching too much TV or playing the whole day etc. Keep improving your skills, abilities and learn from your experiences. Don't blame others and be your own critic. Never let your motivation level drop. You may also find a mentor to help you in ploughing the right path.

Role of Parents in Shaping of a Genius Child

Parents have a great role in shaping a child's greatness. There is a lot that parents can do to encourage their child to become an achiever. The aim should be to help the child to achieve his full potential. The early years are more important as the child picks up the basics of life. During the early stage, parents should remember to do the following:

- Start speaking to the child early and that too, often.
- Get the child take up reading as early as possible. In the initial stage, parents can read books to the child by way of reading story books or reciting poems.
- Nurture the child in a way to arouse his curiosity and development of the brain. Do encourage him to do his own work and this will help him to gain confidence.
- Do set high expectations keeping in mind the child's age and ability. Initially, set targets which are within his reach and once the child gains confidence, set tasks which make him stretch a bit.
- The child must be taught to embrace failure. However,

he must rise to the occasion and work with total dedication and focus. He must believe in taking action and be enthusiastic.

- Encourage in the child a growth mind set. He should not get complacent or start depending on his parents on meeting his daily requirements. He should believe that abilities can be developed. Studies have shown exclusively that mind set, parent nurturing, peers, media, culture, focus and motivation has a profound affect on development of abilities in a child.
- Parents must remember that it takes time and intense effort over a long time to achieve greatness. Mozart's true greatness as a composer developed over a time.

Let your Child Succeed in School

Parents are the most influential people in a child's life. It is a known fact that when parents are involved, children perform better in school. There are several reasons for this. It sends a positive message to your child that you care for his education. It is also true that schools pay more attention to children whose parents are involved because they make their expectations known, so teachers can work towards those expectations. Another important point is that parents come to know about what is being taught. They can help and guide the child to perform much better. As a responsible parent, you could do the following:

- Try to know the syllabus, method of teaching and evaluation system. Also, find out the examination dates so that you can help your child in making a study plan.
- Ensure that your child studies every day. For this, set

aside a particular time for study. Do assist him to finish his homework and also, revise what he had learnt during the day. It is imperative to provide the right environment for study.

- Let the child learn from home the importance of values in life. This will help in shaping his personality and outlook on life. Teach him to be attentive, focused, persistent and have a positive mindset.
- Encourage the child to take part in extra curricular activities at school. He must play at least one game, learn music or dancing, take active part in public speaking, debates or any other facility being provided by the school.
- Lay emphasis on improving reading and writing skills. Keep some books at home and you may join a public library. Parents may ask the child to read from a book and thereafter have a meaningful discussion on the same. Also, child can be given a written assignment which increases his writing skills.
- Limit the time your child spends on watching TV, playing video games and using the cell phone.
- Parents should regularly meet and try to know the class teachers well and school Principal too. They must attend the Parent-Teachers meet. Ask them questions where your child stands and how he is doing. Find out where he needs improvement.

Genes do play a role in the performance of a child, but it is interaction between genes and the environment which produces a genius. So, parents should provide the right environment for the child to improve his intelligence level. Every child should try to develop to be attentive, totally focused in whatever he does. His endeavour should be to excel in his studies. Parents have to help the child to achieve his full potential. They should be encouraging the child to study regularly.

With humility, with hope and extra ordinary determination and development of the mind, greatness is something to which any student can aspire.

24

Be Aware of the Continuous and Comprehensive Evaluation? (CCE)

Let me ask you a question. Are you aware of the salient features of RTE Act? How is the performance of your child going to be evaluated? Are you aware of the Continuous and Comprehensive Evaluation [CCE]? If the answer to any of these questions is 'NO', there is a need for you to have some working knowledge, so that you can help your child to excel in his studies and develop all round personality.

Salient features of RTE Act 2009 are:

- The purpose of RTE Act 2009 is to provide for free and compulsory education to all children of the age of six and fourteen years. The idea is laudable and needs encouragement and support at all levels. The Act lays down duties of the government, local authority and parents. It also includes responsibilities of schools and the teachers.

- The Act directs the academic authority while laying down the curriculum and the evaluation procedures, to take into account the following considerations :-
  - Conformity with the values enshrined in the Constitution.
  - All round development of the child.
  - Building up the child's knowledge, potentiality and talent.
  - Development of physical and mental abilities to the fullest extent.
  - Learning through activities, discovery and exploration in a child friendly and child centred manners.
  - Medium of instructions shall, as possible be in the child's mother tongue.
  - Making the child free of fears, trauma and anxiety and helping the child to express views freely.
  - So, the emphasis is not only on academic excellence but also on development of all round personality of the child.

What is Continuous and Comprehensive Evaluation?

Central Board of Secondary Education (CBSE) has recently introduced the scheme of Continuous and Compulsory Evaluation (CCE) in its schools in a phased manner. From year 2011 onwards, CCE has introduced grades in place of marks for classes 9th and 10th. It has done away with Board Examination for class 10th. This has greatly reduced stress on the students and will definitely produce learners with greater skills. My advice to the parents is that they should try to go through the Teachers' Manual on CCE, published by CBSE.

Copy of this Manual is likely to be available in the school's library. You may also look up the internet for the same. The CCE takes care of scholastic and co-scholastic aspects of a child's learning and growth:

- Scholastic aspects includes curricular areas or subject specific areas. It also covers work experience, art education, and physical and health education.
- Co-Scholastic aspects includes life skills, social skills, thinking skills, emotional skills, co-curricular activities, attitudes and value systems, and different kinds of activities.

Having known what all is included under co- scholastic aspects? The same is shown in the diagram given below:

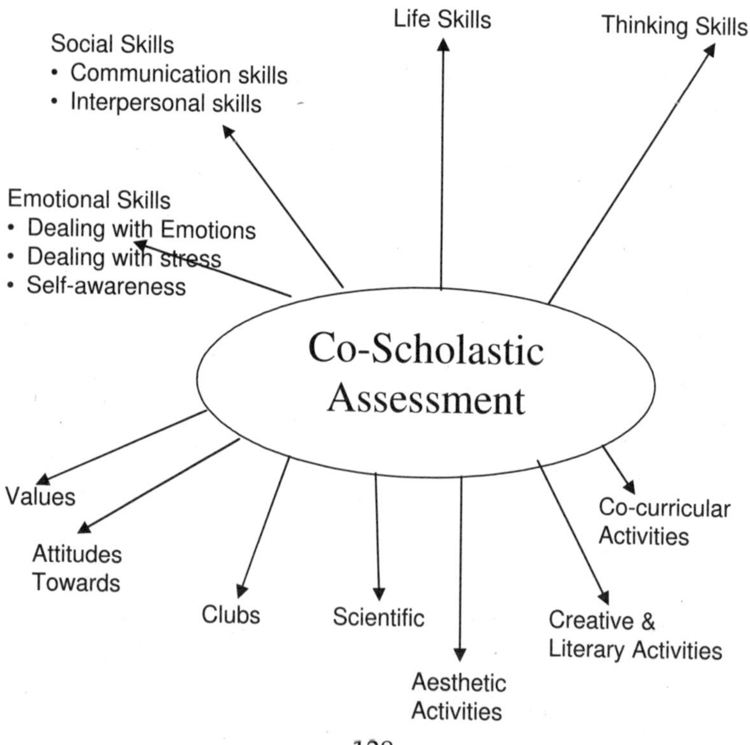

Co- Scholastic Assessment

The evaluation of co-scholastic is based on observation, check lists, anecdotal record and portfolios. It includes, Part 2 and 3 of evaluation card.

Co-scholastic Assessment. Part-2. Consists of co-scholastic area where participants are assessed in two parts: 2[A] Life Skills and 2[B] Attitudes and Values.

- **Part-2 [A].** Life Skills consists of thinking skills, social skills and emotional skills.
- **Part-2 [B].** This consists of attitude towards teachers, schoolmates, school programme and environment.

Co-scholastic Assessment. Part-3. Consists of co-scholastic areas wherein choice is available. This part consists of two sub parts.

- **Part-3[A].** The learner has to choose any two from the following:
  - Writing, Drawing, Poster Making, Slogan Writing, On the Spot Painting, Theatre.
  - Science Club. These skills include; Projects, Maths Club, Science Quiz, Science Exhibition, Olympiads.
  - Aesthetic Literary and Creative Skills. This skills include; Debate, Declamation, Creative Skills. These skills include; Music, Vocal, Instrumental, Dance, Drama, Craft, Sculpture, Puppetry, Folk Art Forms.
  - Clubs. Eco, Health, Wellness and Others.
- **Part-3[B].** Eight different kinds of activities have been provided and the learner has to choose any two. The activities offered include; Sports/Indigenous Sports

[KHO-KHO etc.], NCC/NSS, Scouting and Guiding, Swimming, Gymnastics, Yoga, First Aid, Gardening/ Shramdaan.

Check List- Part 2[A]. Life Skills

Here is a brief on what is included in the Check List of co-scholastic aspects in Part 2 [A].

Thinking Skills—Check List

- Does the student show creativity during class activities? Does she/he accept the challenge enthusiastically?
- Does he/she try to give new ideas or concepts and try to go beyond conditioned setups?
- Does he/she ask questions related to the set task?
- Does he/she create doubts by asking irrelevant things away from the task?
- Does he/she try to help others or motivate others during group activity?
- Does he/she try to volunteer for special assignments?
- Does he/she try different ways of doing a single activity?
- Does he/she like to think out of the box?
- Does he/she try to apply knowledge or skills in new situations?
- Does he/she think about all the possible options for starting a task?

Social Skills—Check List

- Does he/she show patience during a group task for slow learners to complete their task?

- Does he/she try to help a classmate who is feeling low or who's unable to cope up the given work?
- Does he/she appreciate the ideas and qualities of others?
- Does he/she feel comfortable sharing his ideas with others?
- Does the child always like to be appreciated?
- Does he/she come and ask how to correct the mistakes the teacher pointed out in his work?
- Does the student maintain a comfortable level of eye contact?
- Does the student interrupt to tell his own stories/ give his opinion/offers unasked advice?
- Does he/she try to break rules setup for the task by using rude language?
- Does he/she to exhibit negative behaviour and upset others?

Emotional Skills—Check List

- During an activity/competition does the child often says, "I will never win. I'm not just a lucky person?"
- Does he/she choose an activity/task according to his ability during a group work?
- Does he/she scream at the classmates when he is angry or disturbed?
- Does he/she try to do the task again, if declared unsuccessful in the first attempt?
- Does he/she try to improve weaker areas by putting in regular practice?
- Does he/she try to take help of teacher/partner under difficult situations?

- Does he/she to get secluded when under stress?
- Does he/she try to take up some healthy activity like reading, gardening pr playing under stressful time?
- Does he/she become argumentative during discussions?
- Does he/she show disrespect to the system or discipline of the class/school?

Indicators Part-2[B]. Attitudes and Values

Co-scholastic Assessment: Part-2 [B]. This consists of attitude towards teachers, schoolmates, school programme and environment. Given below are Indicators of Assessment for Attitudes and Values. These can be used for writing Descriptive Indicators.

Towards Teachers

- Shows respect and courtesy at all times inside and outside the classroom.
- Demonstrative attitudes that are positive and conducive to learning.
- Takes criticism in the right spirit.
- Respects and follows class teacher and school rules.

Towards School

- Shares a healthy rapport with peers/mates.
- Is able to interact effectively with classmates.
- Is able to express /contribute ideas and opinions in a group.
- Is receptive to ideas and opinions of others in a group.
- Respects and is sensitive to differences among peers in—ability, religious beliefs, gender, culture etc.

- Is kind and helpful.
- Is able to inspire members of the class or peer group.

Toward School Programmes

- Is punctual and regular in attending school programmes.
- Participates and volunteers often for school programmes.
- Delivers a job assigned effectively and responsibly.
- Displays a healthy school spirit.
- Displays leadership skills.
- Inspires others to participate in school programmes.

Towards Environment

- Respects school property.
- Aware of/sensitive to the threats posed to nature by mankind, shows responsibility towards the environment, is environmentally sensitive.
- Participates in school driven activities relating to care for the environment.
- Takes the initiative and plans activities directed towards the betterment of the environment.
- Cares of others, respect life, respect Mother Earth, love for one's own country.

Value Systems

- Understand the need for rules and follows them.
- Honest and ethical exhibits integrity.
- Has self-respect.
- Polite, courteous to everyone.

- Exhibits leadership.
- Respects diversity (culture, opinions, beliefs, abilities), respects the opposite sex.
- Shows a kind, helpful and responsible behaviour/attitude.
- Displays commitment and an open mind.
- Works efficiently, respects time, his/her own and others'.
- Displays a positive attitude towards peers, adults and community, seeks and provides solutions.
- Is a responsible member of the community, displays spirit of citizenship, is conscious of his responsibility towards the community specially the under-privileged members.
- Peace loving; strives for conflict management in all stressful situations.
- Ability to find happiness within oneself.

In a nutshell, it is important both for the parents and the students, to have a good knowledge of CCE and the guidelines for evaluation in the schools. This will help the parents to teach their child various life skills, inculcate values and improve their attitudes towards teachers, school and the environment. In addition, various facilities are being provided to develop all round personality. This book which you are reading, contains valuable information that will assist you to help and guide your child in achieving his full potential. Even students can benefit a lot by reading this self help book. It will help them to excel in studies and will be able to shape a good future for themselves.

25

Improve Your Memory Power

"Memory is the library of the mind"—*Fauvel Gourand*

Wouldn't it be nice to remember what you learn in the school and score high marks in the exams? What if you could never again forget a friend's birthday? Too many students get stuck and convince themselves that their memory is bad, that they are just not good with names and that numbers just slip out of their minds for some reason. Erase these thoughts and vow to improve your memory. Convince yourself that you do have a good memory and that it can be further improved.

If you ever think that genius with good memory can only be born, you can be seriously wrong. In 1952, an experiment was done by Aaron Stern on his daughter, Edith, which proves to the world that given the right environment and strategies, a person's intelligence can be developed and trained. Edith was truly a genius who obtained a Ph.D. degree at the age of 18. In short, Aaron Stern trained Edith from the time she was born. Playing classical music to her, using picture cards and flash cards to teach her everyday even when she was only a few weeks old. At the age of 5, she had finished reading the entire encyclopedia Britannica. The good news is, you can train yourself to be a genius too, even though you started out late. It's only a matter of adopting the right strategies and methods. Improving your memory is the right strategy.

Here is how you can improve your memory.

- **Concentration.**—Concentration means focus of mind. In simple words, concentration is being alert without any diversions in the mind. When you are attentive, you are able to listen and also observe. This helps to remember and recall form the data stored in the brain. It is a known fact that you remember things when you are interested in them. Given below are few exercises to improve you concentration power. Sit straight at a place where there will be no disturbance. You could do one of the following:
  - Count in ascending and descending order, 1 to 100 and thereafter, 100 to 1. Close your eyes, and visualise numbers in green/white/black colour with yellow background.
  - Take a comb and count the number of sticks on it.
  - Inhale and exhale 4 to 5 times. Then count 11, 12,123, 1234-upto 100 and vice versa.
  - Write with left hand for 8 to 10 minutes. Or walk backwards. Helps connection with right brain.
  - Write down names of your friends and recollect their faces and their voice.
  - Recollect taste of 2 to 3 dishes and their smell.
  - Look at 2 to 3 objects for few seconds and close your eyes. Visualise the objects.
  - Visualise what you have done throughout the day, people you met, work you started/finished etc.

- **Association and Images.**—You remember information more easily if you can visualize it. If you want to associate a child with a book, try not to visualize the child reading the book—that's too simple and forgettable. Instead, come up with something more vivid, something that sticks, like the book chasing the child, or the child eating the book. It's your mind that makes the images as shocking and emotional as possible to keep the associations strong. Remember the following when making the images:
  - Always use positive images as your brain often blocks negative ones.
  - Use all your senses to code information.
  - Use vivid, colorful sense –laden images as they are easy to remember.
  - Give your image three dimensions, movement and space to make it more vivid.
- **Use Time and Emotions.**—Do you remember the time when you first saw snowfall? What were your emotions? If you think of the emotions or the time, you will be able to recall the event. Why? Because, time and emotions are strongly connected. So, during examinations, if you forget answer to a question, you try to recollect its memorizing time and your emotion at that point of time. Your chances to recall the answer correctly are increased manifold.
- **Spaced Repetition Learning.**—Revise information you're trying to memorize to yourself every few days or so. This is called spaced repetition learning. We are more likely to remember more recent things and things that we've experienced with greater frequency,

so repeating associations and mnemonics to you is a good idea. Start practicing every day, and you can gradually decrease the frequency until you remember it naturally. Spacing out your studying is important because it gives your brain time to encode the information and store it in your long-term memory.

- **Organize Your Life.**—Keep items that you frequently need, such as keys and eyeglasses, in the same place every time. Use an electronic organizer or daily planner to keep track of things you have to do and other tasks. Keep phone numbers and addresses in an address book or enter them into your computer or cell phone. Improved organization can help you avoid remembering less important things and you can concentrate on the important ones.
- **Recall the Blocked Information.**—Sometimes when you try to recall, you may not be able to recall it at that time even if you are sure that you know it very well. Normally, you tend to try again and again but in vain. To handle this situation you should just keep away from trying to recollect it and do something else. To your pleasant surprise that information automatically pops up into your mind after some time. This is because even if you stopped trying, the mind is searching for that information and brings it to awareness when it is found.

Memory Enhancement Techniques-Mnemonics

Mnemonics means to use artificial aids to remember things. These techniques sharpen the mind and give you an edge over others. You are able to recall quickly and correctly too.

§ **Use of Acronym.** Do you remember the colors of rainbow? Yes! It's VIBGYOR. Here you see that each letter is the first alphabet of the color. For example, V is for violet, I is for indigo and so on.

§ **Rhyme.** Most of us have learnt the number of days in each month by the simple rhyme; "Thirty days hath September........."

§ **Using Cues.** Let's say you want to buy apples and you have forgotten about it. When you go out for shopping, you can look at the fruits and use them as a cue. This will remind you that you have to buy apples.

§ **Chunking.** When you group information together to help you remember them; it's called chunking. Random lists of things (a shopping list, for example) can be especially difficult to remember. To make it easier, try categorizing the individual things from the list. If you can remember that, among other things, you wanted to buy four different kinds of vegetables, you'll find it easier to remember all four.

§ **Make a Phrase.** The reason that most of us can't remember our friend's phone number is because 535-3473 is just a string of numbers that have no obvious connection to your friend. In order to use your memory efficiently, the best way is to actively create an association for things you're trying to remember. For example, write out your friend's phone number: five three five three four seven three. Now try to create a clever phrase that starts with the first letter of those words: "fairy tales feel true for some time." You're now much more likely to remember that phone number.

§ **Tell a Story.** If you have to remember some things, you can transform the material into visible images or use it to tell a story. Let us say you want to remember that coal is found in Ranganj. You can visualize that is coal is burning on the head of Rani Mukerjee and she has gone ganji (bald).

§ **Roof Top Method.** If something you want to remember, try to make sense of it and then you can transform the material into visual images. If you want to memorize the answer to a question which is long or in point form, you can use roof top method. You can visualize that you are standing on a roof top and create a picture/scene which includes all the elements/things, you want to memorize.

§ **Increasing Vocabulary.** To increase your vocabulary, you need to learn new words. Look at the word and try to find an odd word in it, for example, 'Asinine'. It means 'stupid'. What's the odd word in the word, 'Ass nine'! You can now make sentence, "Nine asses are roaming stupidly in the fields. Now try the word 'Cajole', it means "to flatter."

Exercise Your Brain

Scientists believe that it is the physical formation of the brain that determines a person's intelligence. The ability of the brain to function is based greatly on the ability of its neurons to connect with each other. How can one increase the connection of neurons? By continuing to exercise the brain through reading and solving academic puzzles, playing memory video games etc, anyone can increase and maintain their brain powers. Neurons connection can be increased by:-

- **Exercise Daily.** Regular aerobic exercise improves circulation and efficiency throughout the body, including the brain. It can help to ward off the memory loss that comes with aging. Exercise also makes you more alert and relaxed, and can thereby improve your memory uptake.
- **Breathing Pattern.** When you want to study or remember something new, switch your breathing pattern to be slower and deeper. Deeper and slower breathing from the abdomen actually changes the way your brain works. It indices the brain's electrical pulses to switch to Theta waves. It turns out that being at this stage, helps in aid to memory.
- **Reduce Stress.** Chronic stress physically damages the brain, and it can make remembering much more difficult. After prolonged stress, the brain will start to become affected and deteriorate. Realistically speaking, stress may never be completely eliminated from one's life, but it definitely can be controlled.
- **Eat Well and Eat Right.** A healthy diet, contributes to a healthy brain, and foods containing antioxidants like broccoli, blueberries, spinach, berries, and Omega-3 fatty acids appear to promote healthy brain functioning. Feed your brain with such supplements as, Thiamine, Niacin and Vitamin-B 6.

Take a Memory Exercise

Let us say that you want to memorize something new. How would you go about it? Write it down on a piece of paper or in your note book. Time for consideration is 5 minutes.

Suggested Methodology

- When you want to learn something new, pay full attention. There should not be any distraction or letting your mind wander. You need to concentrate, focus and tell your brain that this information is important and worth storing later.
- Know your learning style. You could attach visual or auditory cues to the important part of the information. You could make your own connections to things you already know. These connections could at times be silly, but must help you to understand the subject matter and also assist in its easy recall.
- Make full use of your sensory inputs. It could be by touch or by smell, where you can use a particular scent. Thinking and feeling about that scent it will help in connecting with the brain, and you can easily recall the required the information.
- You may write down as you read or once you finish, as the brain connects better to the new information.

You could write down again what you have learnt, after some time. Even flash cards would be of considerable help to revise.

26

Thinking Skills

"What we think we become."
—Buddha

A good student should be able to think clearly and arrive at a workable solution after considering all aspects of the given problem. Thinking skills comprises of self awareness, creative thinking, critical thinking, problem solving and decision making. A student should show creativity during class activities and accept challenges with enthusiasm. He should think out of the box and give new ideas or concepts. He is expected to apply knowledge and skills in new situations and think about all the possible options before under taking a task.

Parents have a great role in empowering their child with creative and critical thinking skills. This will not only make him intelligent and smart, but will also make him successful in whatever career he wants to pursue. Here are some ideas and suggestions to help encourage thinking skills in your child:

- Encourage your child to ask a series of questions, even if they sound very silly and strange. Try to answer them to the best of your abilities without losing your patience.

- Be enthusiastic while answering questions. Show your child, that you are caring towards his concerns and questions.
- The child should feel that he or she is being listened to. As a parent, your duty must start at satisfying your child's curiosity and inquisitiveness.
- Why, Where, What and How type of questions will make your child, develop a number of critical thinking skills.
- Your child must be able to think and analyze whether a given set of information is really true or not. Once he learns to differentiate the right from the wrong, you can be rest assured that he or she will start looking at things, events, and scenarios with a probing angle.
- Never ever answer all questions on your own. Sometimes, encourage your child to answer few questions on his own.

Creative Thinking

Creativity is partly a frame of mind. You need to expand your mind's capabilities, that is, open yourself up to new ideas. You can be more effective at solving problems creatively, if you use the following suggestions:

- Think of yourself as creative. Believing in your ability to be creative is the first step in becoming more creative.
- Pay attention to your intuition. Every individual has a subconscious mind that works well. Sometimes answers will come when you least expect them.
- Move away from your comfort zone. Every individual has a comfort zone in which certainty exists. To be

creative, you need to move away from the status quo and focus your mind on something new.

- Determine what you want to do. This includes taking time to understand the problem, getting all the facts, and identify the most important facts.
- Think outside the box. Use different problem-solving strategies such as verbal, visual, mathematical, or theatrical. Look at your problem from a different perspective.
- Look for ways to do things better. This may involve trying consciously to be original, keeping an open mind, discarding usual or habitual ways of doing things, and striving for objectivity.
- Believe in finding a workable solution. Like believing in yourself, you also need to believe in your ideas.
- Turn creative ideas into action. Coming up with creative ideas is only part of the process. Once the ideas are generated, they must be implemented.

Critical Thinking

Can critical thinking skills be improved? The simple answer is yes. We all learn at different rates and in different ways. In other words, developing critical thinking skills takes more time for some than others. What is important is the desire and willingness to learn and stretch past your comfort zone. This stretching will expand your knowledge base, and help you with developing critical thinking skills.

Key Elements of Critical Thinking

- **A Curious and Open Mind.** A childlike fascination with the world and an open mind about it is a powerful combination. Each experience provides one more piece of the amazingly complex puzzle of life. For every challenge undertaken, whether a win or a loss, a success or a failure; invaluable experience is gained. For the critical thinker, education doesn't stop at high school, or college. Learning is a lifelong commitment. Bernard Baruch is of the view, "Millions saw the apple fall, but Newton was the one who asked why?"

- **Thinking Through Issues.** Developing critical thinking skills encourages digging deeper into issues and challenges. This is done by thinking through an objective. First, facts and data are gathered. Then, assumptions and risks are considered. Finally, an informed decision is made and appropriate action is taken to achieve a goal. This systematically process is known as a stream of logic. The more critical the challenge, the more thinking is required. Here is one example of how the thinking through process works.

Sir Edmund Hillary and Tenzing Norgay were the first to successfully climb Mount Everest and return alive. Hillary paid close attention to the smallest details. For example, he invested a full day checking oxygen cylinders and determining flow rates (gathering facts and data). He understood that carefully thinking through their objective could be the difference between life and death. Having enough oxygen to make the round trip would be essential (assumption) because it was critical for survival (risk). Due to his understanding of the oxygen needs for the journey ahead and always observant, Hillary spotted half-empty oxygen bottles along the way. He decided to pick them up for later use. After Hillary and Norgay reached the summit of Mt. Everest, they changed their almost empty oxygen bottles with the bottles they had picked up. This got them safely back to camp. Critical thinking skills not only helped them reach the summit, it may have saved their lives too. Sir Edmund Hillary rightly said, "It is not the mountain we conquer but ourselves."

- **Analyze Issues from Multiple View Points.** Almost all issues can be looked at several ways. Different perspectives (also known as view points) help provide better solutions to issues. Opening up to see multiple sides of an issue is a powerful skill. There are significant benefits to looking at multiple view points. You are able to find the best solution to a problem. Common questions to ask yourself are:
  - Are there other perspectives that I can view this from?
  - What are these other view points?
  - How can I use these perspectives to resolve this challenge?
  - Do I understand the cause and effect of decisions made, or actions taken?

Problem Solving

A problem means that the thing is happening which is a deviation to what should actually happen. Problem solving is a process of taking corrective action to meet objectives. A problem needs to be dealt with an open mind. Initially, carryout analysis of the situation by breaking down the problem in smaller parts. Thereafter, structure your findings. This helps in making sense of the complex problems. It allows us to compare and weigh relevant element with another. Here are few creative problem solving techniques:

- **Problem Re-statement.** The aim is to broaden our perspective. It helps in, identifying central issues and alternative solutions. This increases chances of arriving at an outcome which resolves the problem.
- **SWOT Analysis.** It is a simple but powerful frame work for analyzing an organization's strength and weaknesses, and the opportunities and threats it faces. This helps the organization to focus on the strengths, minimize threats and take the greatest possible advantage of the available opportunities.
- **Pareto's Principle.** Also known as 80/20 Rule. This argues that typically 80% of unfocused effort produces 20% of results. The remaining 80% is achieved by 20 of the effort. So focus on important issues for better results.
- **Brain Storming.** It is a great way of generating radical ideas. During the brain storming session there is no criticism of ideas. Thereafter, ideas are considered to generate best possible outcome.
- **Ask 'Why' Five Times.** When you have a problem, ask "why". You are likely to get an answer, to that again ask "why". This way, ask "why" five times. Well, you may be surprised that invariably a possible solution emerges.
- **Six Universal Questions.** Sometimes, asking the six universal questions can lead to solve a problem. The six universal questions are; WHAT, WHEN WHERE, HOW, WHY, WHO.

Decision Making

Decision making is a process of selecting an alternative course of action that will solve the problem. The 7 Decision Making Steps shown here can be used in a wide array of personal and professional decision making. They can be also be used for deciding where to go on a vacation, selecting a mobile you want to buy, and a wide array of other important decisions that you must make.

Step 1: Gather Facts and Data. The first of the steps used to make an informed decision is to gather the facts and data.

Step 2: Make Assumptions. The assumptions used while making a decision are important. Ask the following questions about your assumptions:

- Are your assumptions valid?
- If so, why?
- If not, why not?

Step 3: Identify Options. Once you have identified the options that are available, move to the next decision making step.

Step 4: Use Logic and Common Sense. Combine your logic and common sense with the facts and data, assumptions, knowledge and experience. Ask yourself questions like:

- Does this decision make sense?
- If so, why?
- If not, why not?

Step 5: Incorporate Feelings. Many people use their feelings and emotions to make most, if not all of their decisions. They ask themselves questions such as: Do I like its color, shape, texture and/or feel of this product? Feelings are an important part of any decision. However, they need to be backed up by knowledge, logic and common sense when using these decision making steps.

Step 6: Make Decision. Two primary types of decisions are:

- A yes or no decision. For example should you buy a house or continue to rent. Another example is should you change a particular subject.
- Selecting from options available. Which options should be selected? For example, Vijay had options to select the type of model when he was choosing a car.

Step 7: Modify or Change Decision. Frequently, new facts and data become available after you have made a decision. Sometimes this information will be relatively significant and important. If the new information would have changed your mind if received earlier, then you can modify or change your decision. If your decision is difficult to change, then determine a way to handle it. Change it in the future if possible.

In a nutshell, there should be greater emphasis on

thinking skills than on rote learning. The focus should be to measure student's abilities to reason, justify, analyze process and evaluate information. The aim should be to use the knowledge acquired to real life situations. Apart from the school, parents can play a great role in development and refine the thinking skills of their children.

QUOTES ON THINKING SKILLS

Those who know how to think need no teacher

—Mahatma Gandhi

No problem can withstand onslaught of sustained thinking

—Voltaire

A man, who does not think for himself, does not think at all

—Oscar Wilde

If everybody is thinking alike, then somebody is not thinking

—George S Patton

Thinking is one thing, which no one has been able to tax

—Charles Kettering

The world we have created is a product of our thinking, it can not be changed without changing our thinking

—Albert Einstein

Bibliography

Books

Dare to Win by Jack Canfield & Mark Victor.

How to Win Friends and Influence People by Dale Carnegie.

Rich Dad Poor Dad by Robert T Kiyosaki.

The Secret by Rhonda Byrne.

The Success Principles by Jack Canfield.

The Seven Spiritual Laws of Success: The Secret to Wealth by Napoleon Hill.

The Seven Habits of Highly Effective People by Stephen R Covey.

Wings of Fire: An Autobiography of A P J Abdul Kalam by Arun Tiwari.

The Monk Who Sold His Ferrari by Robin S Sharma.

Teachers Manual on CCE published by the CBSE Board.

Websites

http://www.culturalindia.net

http://www.mediabharti.com

http//www.moralsandethics.wordpress.com

http//www.poweract.blogspot.com

http//www.successconsciousness.com